EDWARDIAN RAILWAYS
IN POSTCARDS

26 DOVER. — Ostend Boat at Pier. — LL.

JOHN HANNAVY

First published in 2017

A CIP catalogue record for this book is available from the British Library.

John Hannavy has asserted his right under the Copyright, Designs and Patents Act 1988 to be identified as the author of this book.

ISBN 978 0 85710 115 0

PiXZ Books
Halsgrove House, Ryelands Business Park, Bagley Road, Wellington, Somerset TA21 9PZ
Tel: 01823 653777
Fax: 01823 216796
email: sales@halsgrove.com

An imprint of Halstar Ltd, part of the Halsgrove group of companies
Information on all Halsgrove titles is available at: www.halsgrove.com

Printed and bound in India by Parksons Graphics

Front cover image: This 1904 postcard captioned 'She's a Lassie from Lancashire' was posted from Blackpool on 30 July 1908. It was not actually photographed in Lancashire, but almost certainly in Yorkshire, and at least one variant of the card was captioned 'Arrived Safely at the Mumbles', suggesting that there may have been many other 'localised' versions of it. It was published as part of the 'Coronation Series' of humorous cards.

Title page image: Passengers disembarking from the London to Dover train to board the steamer to Ostend c.1905. This being a Léon & Lévy postcard, it was printed in France.

Contents page image: A composite postcard from the London & North Western Railway, published in 1905, including what was then their latest introduction — the American Vestibule Express, in other words, corridor coaches. These had been commonplace in America for decades, but were only introduced into Britain in the early years of the twentieth century. Also featured on the card were the Euston Arch, one of the company's latest 4-4-0 express locomotives, Liverpool's Landing Stage, and Stephenson's *Rocket*.

All Victorian and Edwardian images are either © John Hannavy Image Library or come from private collections.

By the same author, also published by PiXZ:
• *Preserved Steam-Powered Machines*
• *Edwardian Mining In Old Postcards*
• *The Once-Ubiquitous Paddle-Steamer*
• *Britain's Industrial Heritage*
• *Our Industrial Past — Britain's Industrial Heritage 2*
• *Industries Which Made Britain Triumph — Britain's Industrial Heritage 3*

CONTENTS

INTRODUCTION

I NEVER ACTUALLY SET OUT to be a postcard collector. In fact I never set out to be any sort of collector, but nonetheless collections of Victorian and Edwardian ephemera have increasingly surrounded me for my entire adult life.

The origins of the picture postcard as we know it today can be traced back to the 1870s when a relaxation of postal regulations in mainland Europe permitted private companies to start marketing pictorial cards. In Britain, however, the authorities merely sanctioned the use of plain white cards.

It was not until May 1890 – fifty years after the introduction of the Penny Post and postage stamps – that the first illustrated cards appeared, and those were specifically produced for and by the postal authorities themselves.

Along with the introduction of the plain card – message on one side, address on the other – the Post Office set the postal rate at just a halfpenny, a low cost which would later help drive the popularity of the picture postcard. That rate survived until the end of the First World War.

opposite: Detail from a postcard of the Excursion Platforms on Blackpool's Talbot Road Station which were only used during the summer holidays when thousands visited the resort each week.

below: Railway companies used postcards for self-promotion – the London & North Western Railway claiming that by 1905 more than five million of their promotional cards had been sold. The majority of them were sold to postcard collectors.

5

right: Sunningdale Station — now in Berkshire since boundary changes — was opened in 1856 by the London & South Western Railway. At least three postcards are known to have been produced in the Edwardian era in which the closed level crossing gates formed a visual barrier to seeing the station. There was even a sepia close-up postcard view of the gates themselves. How far down your list of 'must send' postcards would a picture of closed level crossing gates be today?

The Sunningdale Station, Windlesham, Surrey.

A further four and a half years passed before private publishers were allowed to enter the market, and the earliest so far identified – E. T. W. Dennis of Scarborough – produced their first picture cards in 1894 and became one of the country's biggest postcard publishers.

Five years elapsed before the standard format was agreed in November 1899 and, from then onwards, the market for pictorial postcards grew both rapidly and exponentially.

When pictorial cards were first sanctioned, the old rule still applied – message on one face, address on the other – so a white space for a brief message was left beneath the photograph. In 1902, Britain became the first country to approve 'divided back' postcards – message on the left, address on the right – the format which endures to this day.

below: The Highland Railway locomotive *Skibo Castle* was one of a batch of nineteen 4-6-0 tender engines designed by Peter Drummond and built between 1900 and 1917. Ten were built by Dübs & Co. with nine being built at the North British Locomotive Works. No.146 was delivered by Dübs in 1902. *Skibo Castle* remained in service under LMS colours — and carrying the number 14681 — until 1946.

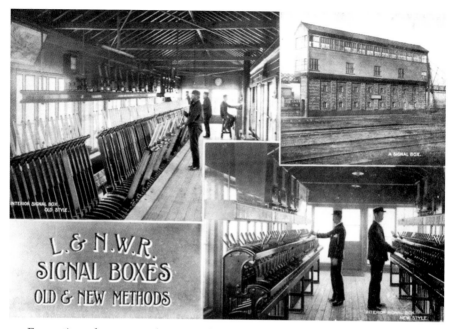

L. & N.W.R.
SIGNAL BOXES
OLD & NEW METHODS

For a time, however, that new freedom imposed a new restriction – until other countries adopted the protocol, British divided back cards could not be posted overseas, and were therefore of no use to foreign tourists visiting Britain.

As a photographic historian, my interests lie primarily in photo-based cards, so the many artists' impressions of speeding expresses will not be found on these pages – the photographic process was still somewhat limited in Edwardian times when it came to 'action' pictures.

Photographically-illustrated postcards probably first appeared in Britain in late 1900 or early 1901, by which time postcard collecting was already sufficiently well established as a hobby for there to be a dedicated magazine for enthusiasts – *The Picture Postcard Magazine of Philately, Travel & Art* first appeared in July 1900, changing its name two years later to *Picture Postcard and Collectors' Chronicle*.

By 1900 there was even a dedicated publisher – The Locomotive Publishing Company. Their first cards were printed in monochrome, but within four years, they and other publishers were using colour lithography to produce cards of very high quality.

above: Another of the London & North Western Railway's 1905 'official' postcards sought to promote the company as being at the leading edge of technological development. Despite the card illustrating the traditional lever frame signal box as being 'old style' technology – illustrating its power-frame successor as the future – such manually-operated boxes continue in use on some lines to this day. The L&NWR's 180-lever mechanical box at Severn Bridge Junction, opened in 1904, is the largest still working in Europe.

below: Francis William Webb designed the 'Precedent' Class 2-4-0 locomotive — of which *Charles Dickens* was one of the most famous — for the London & North Western Railway, initially building ninety engines at the Crewe Works between 1874 and 1882. *Charles Dickens* was one of the last, and from 1882 until withdrawn from service in 1912, the locomotive travelled more than 2,300,000 miles on the network. A single example of the later 'Improved' Precedent Class, *Hardwicke* built in 1892, is preserved in the National Railway Museum in York.

Early 'peopled' postcards were invariably posed, and that, of course, implies a certain willing complicity on the part of all the people who feature in these views. They were, in the main, more than happy to have their own little bit of fame, and probably thoroughly enjoyed seeing themselves staring out from the counter of station news-stands.

Postcards were produced in enormous numbers in the Edwardian era — some sources say in excess of 500,000,000 annually — to meet a seemingly insatiable demand, so no aspect of railway life was considered too trivial to be featured. They give us a colourful picture of life back then.

The idea of buying a postcard while waiting at the railway station, and writing a brief message to a friend before boarding the train may seem alien to us today, but a hundred years ago, it was commonplace. Almost every station sold postcard views of its platforms, its staff and the trains which stopped there.

A century ago, in the days before everyone carried a telephone, and at a time when the post office collected and delivered mail several times a day, the picture postcard was the equivalent of today's text message, the quickest and most reliable way of simply saying 'I'm home safely', or making arrangements to contact a friend — the monochrome card on

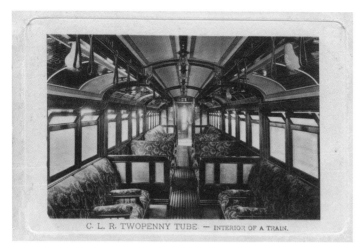

C. L. R. TWOPENNY TUBE — INTERIOR OF A TRAIN.

left: The interior of a Central London Railway tube train car, from a postcard published c.1902. It took eleven years from setting up the company in 1889 before the CLR began operating services for the first time in 1900. Its tunnels are still in use today and form part of the Central Line.

page 11, posted in Ilford at noon on 10 June 1905, carries the message 'If convenient, 7pm Ilford Station.'.

With many cards to choose from, the sender could pick one to suit a mood, an occasion, or a memory. In addition to the expected range of scenic cards – and a vastly wider range than any town or city can offer today – every stationer sold humorous postcards, romantic ones, cards which told stories, carried the words of songs, and many others.

Every W. H. Smiths or John Menzies bookstall on the station platform offered railway cards. Through them we can get a wonderful picture of life and work on the railways more than a century ago.

At usually no more than a halfpenny for a simple monochrome card – and often as little as an old penny for a coloured view – and a halfpenny to post it, the postcard was the communication medium for everyman.

Chromo-lithography, or chromographic printing, had been around for a long time before the picture postcard, but the introduction of cards based on photographs presented manufacturers with considerable and time-consuming challenges if they sought to give their tinted cards any semblance of realism – the subtle tones of the photograph had to be preserved, and coloured hues had to look natural. As an example, the tinted card of the South East & Chatham Railway's Boat-Train, *page 11*, was derived from the same monochrome photograph as the card below it.

right: Many local stationers became postcard publishers themselves, as well as stocking cards produced by the larger publishers including E.T.W Dennis, Raphael Tuck, Wrench, and many others. This postcard advertised Will Smith's shop on Wigan Lane, Wigan, Lancashire – no relation to his namesake, the much more famous William Henry Smith. Wigan's Will Smith advertised himself as 'The Postcard King' and is known to have published several dozen different views of the town and its workforce.

THE POST-CARD KING.

The Largest and Best Selection in Wigan.

Wholesale and Retail.

"Always Something New."

26 & 28, Wigan Lane, WIGAN.

Telephone 249.

below: A range of railway postcards would have been on sale at W.H.Smith's bookstall on the platforms of every railway station. London's Marylebone Station, seen here in a postcard c.1904, was then London's newest terminus, having only been opened in 1899 to serve the Great Central Railway's route to Leicester, Sheffield and Manchester Central.

Many of the best tinted Edwardian cards were produced in Germany, where the quality of colour lithographic printing had been raised to a much higher standard – and at a much lower cost – than could be found in Britain.

German cards were considered to be 'quality' items! Even large American postcard publishers chose to have their cards printed in Europe – using printers in both Germany and Holland – in order to achieve the highest standards.

Each colour and each tint was created from a separate litho stone overprinted onto the monochrome card – a complex process resulting in a premium product for which the public seemed willing to pay a premium price.

While quite realistic effects could be created with three or four separate printings, the finest chromo-lithographic cards

Great Central Railway Station, Marylebone.

"THE BOAT-TRAIN", S. E. & CHATHAM RLY.

The Knight Series, No. 984.

"THE BOAT TRAIN", S. E. & CHATHAM RLY.

The Knight Series, No. 601.

above & left: Two 'Knight Series' cards from around 1904 showing the SE&CR's 1901-built Wainwright D Class 4-4-0 locomotive No.728 at the head of the boat train to Dover. The locomotive was the third of ten in a class of 51 to be built in Glasgow by Sharp, Stewart & Company at their Atlas Works in Springburn. Ten others were built by Dübs & Company at Queens Park Works in Polmadie, Glasgow, five each by Stephenson & Co. in Newcastle and Vulcan Foundry in Newton-le-Willows, Lancashire, with the other 21 built at the SE&CR's Ashford Works in Kent.

could be the result of a dozen or more printings, each carefully applied in perfect register one on top of the other. That often meant that the most attractive postcards cost more to buy than the ha'penny they cost to post – a very different situation to today.

Public enthusiasm for all things German changed with the advent of the Great War, of course. For the duration of the war, the purchase of remaining stock of pre-1914 cards which bore the legend 'Printed at our Works in Bavaria' or 'Printed in Saxony' was positively frowned upon as being unpatriotic

right: This Knight Series postcard shows one of Peter Drummond's Class A 'Castle' 4-6-0 locomotives pulling the 'Highland Mail'. Evolved from the David Jones-designed 'Jones Goods' 2-6-0, the powerful engines could tackle the Highland Railway's steepest gradients.

THE HIGHLAND MAIL (1,484 FEET ABOVE SEA LEVEL).

The Knight Series, No. 608.

below: Many humorous cards focused on the presumed 'goings-on' which took place in railway carriages in the years before corridor trains became the norm.

– with these beautiful productions going from 'must have' to 'must not have' almost overnight! Perhaps that is why so many of them have found their way into collections today without ever having been written on or posted.

Production of the postcard went through several distinct phases before 'real photograph' cards gained popularity. The photographic process, initially, by its time-consuming nature, was ill-suited to large production runs.

For extended print runs, photogravure, lithography and chromo-lithography were the most cost-effective.

For shorter print runs, colour was sometimes added by hand by teams of girls using colour washes, each responsible for a single colour – a practice which would continue to be used occasionally on 'real photograph' cards into the 1920s.

Railways celebrated their own success through postcards – new locomotives were regularly

All tickets please!

photographed for the postcard market, and every railway company produced its own sets of cards – both to advertise and promote the destinations to which they travelled, and to celebrate the achievements of the railways themselves.

As an example, the Crewe-built 'Jumbo' No.955 *Charles Dickens* was given a fresh coat of paint and rolled out for the cameras in late 1904 to commemorate it having travelled well over two million miles – a record for a steam engine which has, apparently, never been equalled, let alone beaten!

In contrast to the bland postcards available today, the Edwardians could choose from an engaging range of postcards in just about every town and village.

below: The Travelling Post Office as seen on two L&NWR official postcards, published in 1904. The idea of letters being sorted in transit on a moving train is almost as old as the railways themselves – the first such service being inaugurated on the Liverpool & Manchester Railway in 1830, allegedly in a converted horse-box. Other railway companies followed with the passing of the Railways (Conveyance of Mails) Act of 1838 which required railways to carry mail – by ordinary or special trains – as required by the Postmaster General. Some had as many as five post office coaches to deal with the volume of post. The first exclusively postal train was the Great Western Railway's service between London and Bristol, inaugurated on 1 February 1855. The apparatus for picking up and setting down mailbags while the train hurtled by at speed had first been installed at two points on the GWR line – at Slough and Maidenhead – as early as 1866. The last mail train ran in early January 2004 ending a service with a history going back more than 130 years.

PICKING UP MAIL BAGS AT FULL SPEED

INTERIOR OF TRAVELLING POST OFFICE.

below right:
Another of the L&NWR's historical cards showing the permanent way in the years before wooden sleepers became the norm.

bottom: L&NWR platelayers at work on tracks just north of London.

At the time these cards were published, the L&NWR's advertised their postcards of 'Engines, Trains, Steamers & Scenery' in packets of six for just two old pennies.

Of course, there were a lot of bland ones as well, but there was sufficient choice to ensure that if you were contacting a friend several times a month, then the chances of duplicating a card could be minimised.

Some of the bland cards were very bland indeed – closed level crossing gates obscuring the view beyond, for example – but they presumably sold in sufficient numbers to be commercially worthwhile.

In addition to many of the spectacular cards which were marketed, no collection would be complete without a selection of the truly banal offerings. Stations with little more than a small shelter on the platform, and perhaps no more

OLD PERMANENT WAY ON STONE BLOCKS, WINSFORD.

Great Eastern Express to Yarmouth

than a handful of trains a day still, apparently, had to have their own postcards.

Often defying any business logic, these cards were printed abroad by colour lithography, requiring large print runs to keep the cost of an individual card at an affordable level. Like the railway lines for which they were produced, their publishers rarely saw any return on their investment.

above: The Great Eastern Railway's line to Yarmouth Vauxhall was opened by the Yarmouth & Norwich Railway in 1844, the line passing to the Eastern Counties Railway in 1848 and the GER when that grouping was formed in 1862.

left: This L&NWR bus, with Dodson bodywork on a Daimler chassis, was exhibited at the 1905 British International Motor Show, held at Olympia. The L&NWR was one of the first companies to regularly use buses and ran an hourly service between Harrow & Wealdstone and Watford Stations.

L.& N.W. MOTOR OMNIBUS.—EXHIBITED AT THE MOTOR EXHIBITION, LONDON, NOVEMBER.1905

Cheeky little hussy!
No one would have to kiss me like that.

Whereas today's postcard market is aimed squarely at the holidaymaker or day visitor, Edwardian cards were aimed just as directly at those who lived and worked throughout the country and, of course, the railways they used regularly.

While today's cards use photographs which exclude anything which might date them and limit their longevity, the publishers of Edwardian postcards revelled in showing local people going about their daily lives – workers practicing their trades and professions as well as enjoying whatever leisure time they had. An obvious aid to sales – who could have possibly resisted buying cards in which they themselves featured prominently?

Southwold Station, at the eastern end of the little branch line which ran from Halesworth to the Suffolk resort, was not unique. There you could buy cards of the goods yard and the station buildings, and the delightful card illustrated here with the entire station staff and the train crew posing proudly by the side of the locomotive. A hundred years after it was produced, this card epitomises the charm of the Edwardian branch line station.

The beautifully tinted views of crowded platforms at Blackpool, Morecambe, Brighton and elsewhere were typical of the bustle which attended the annual migration to Britain's coast for the summer holiday, while others attest to the huge numbers who used the railways daily when going to and from their work.

As people in Edwardian times invariably returned to the same resort in the same week year after year, imagine the delight on returning, to recognise oneself in a new postcard on sale at the station bookstall or in the town's stationers!

Friends back home would surely have enjoyed receiving a card with a figure circled and the legend 'this is me' pencilled in. Many cards carried messages such as 'I'll be home by lunchtime tomorrow' or 'meet me at 7', the sender confident that the card would arrive before he or she did!

Postcards also commemorated railway failures, with disaster postcards often being produced very quickly after a major accident and sold to raise small sums of money to support the bereaved and injured.

opposite top: Southwold Station was opened in 1879 and the 3ft. gauge branch line from Halesworth operated for fifty years before the route was abandoned in 1929.

opposite bottom: One of the many comic railway cards published in the years before the Great War.

below: The scene at Dover's Admiralty Pier from a postcard c.1908. The paddle steamer is either *Dover*, *Calais* or *Lord Warden* all three of which were originally built for the London, Chatham & Dover Railway, while the locomotive is a Wainwright D Class 4-4-0 built at the company's Ashford Works in early 1902. No.740 continued in service well into the British Railways era carrying the number 71740, only being scrapped in 1951. One example of the class — No.737 (BR No.71737) — is preserved at the National Railway Museum.

right: The London, Brighton & South Coast Railway's Brighton to London Victoria express jumped the points as it approached Stoats Nest and Cane Hill Station on January 29 1910, splitting in two. The train's rear three coaches crashed into the platform killing seven people and injuring sixty-five others, eight of them seriously. Local photographers and stationers Batchelder Brothers of Croydon were on hand that night to take a series of flashlight photographs as the wreckage was cleared. These were on sale as postcards within days of the accident. Three years earlier, at the same station, a film cameraman was crushed to death when a locomotive ran over him. In 1911, the station's name was changed to Coulsdon North.

above right: On July 12 1913, an express train from Cromer to London, ran into the back of another locomotive at Colchester Station due to a signalling error. The express train's driver, fireman and guard were all killed. This photo-composite postcard was produced and published by Warner Gothard of Barnsley.

A number of these were produced by Warner Gothard and Sons of Barnsley who, starting with the Cudworth accident in January 1905, developed quite a market for their photo-composite 'disaster' cards, covering industrial and mining accidents as well as major incidents on the railways.

Their last railway disaster card was of the Great Western Railway accident at Reading Station in June 1914 when the driver was killed and two firemen were injured.

Other photographers picked up the idea – a significant example being the Boat Train crash at Salisbury on Sunday 1 July 1906 when the speeding train from Plymouth to Waterloo left the rails, tipped over on to its side, and crashed

top: On 17 September 1912 the 17.30 express from Chester to Liverpool was signalled to cross from the fast line to the slow line at Ditton Junction near Widnes, but the inexperienced driver, unaware of a 15mph speed limit across the points, entered the junction at an estimated 60mph. The driver, fireman and 13 passengers were killed — and a further 50 injured — when the train left the rails, hit a bridge pier, broke up and burst into flames. The London & North Western Railway train was fitted with gas-lighting and the crash had shattered some of the gas cylinders, resulting in an inferno.

above left: One of many postcards published in the days following the Salisbury Boat Train disaster. The London & South Western Railway express from Plymouth Friary to London Waterloo, hauled by a new L&SWR Class L12 4-4-0 locomotive, had reportedly approached the sharp curve at the eastern end of Salisbury Station — which had a speed limit of 30 mph — while travelling at more than 70 mph.

into a milk train on the adjacent track. 28 people died — including two of the crew from the milk train – and 11 were seriously injured.

By dawn that Sunday morning, the first photographers were on the scene, and postcards were on sale in local shops by the end of the week!

Safety on the railways during the period covered by this book was especially bad with no fewer than thirty-four fatal railway accidents and four non-fatal incidents between 23 March 1900 – when four people were killed in an accident when two 19-coach workmen's trains collided in a tunnel near Glasgow's Charing Cross Station – and 17 December

Wemyss Bay Pier.

above: Wemyss Bay Station — designed by James Miller — was opened by the Caledonian Railway in 1903, replacing the Greenock & Wemyss Bay Railway's 1865 station. Now a 'Category A' listed building, it is in great need of restoration. At the pier is the 1890-built steamer PS *Marchioness of Bute*.

right: The Midland Railway's new steamer TS *Londonderry* — built by Denny Bros of Dumbarton and seen here off Morecambe — was introduced on the service between Heysham and Belfast in 1904.

1915 when nineteen died and eighty-one were injured at St Bede's Junction near Jarrow.

In those fifteen years, 550 people lost their lives and more than 1500 were injured. During that period there were only two years – 1902 and 1908 – which were fatal accident-free.

1915 was the worst year – four incidents resulting in 265 deaths and more than 850 injuries. The Quintinshill collision near Gretna Green accounted for 226 of those deaths, with 246

injured, while the accident at Ilford in Essex left ten dead and more than 500 hurt.

By the Edwardian era, the major railway companies had expanded their operations to embrace hotels and the operation of fleets of steam ships – both for travellers to Europe and operating excursion services around Britain's coast and on lakes and lochs.

Railway companies had been allowed to run their own ships since 1863 and by the early 1900s many of them were operating integrated timetables, ensuring that passengers could experience a seamless progression from train to boat.

In the north-west, the Furness Railway's services ranged from excursion steamers on the English Lakes, to scheduled sailings linking Barrow with Blackpool and several other coastal ports.

In Scotland, steamers were an essential part of the transport infrastructure, especially on the west coast which remained largely inaccessible by railway. The Caledonian Railway set up its own shipping line in 1888 – The Caledonian Steam Packet Company – in direct competition to the established operations of David MacBrayne, and built up a fine fleet of paddle steamers to operate its services.

The railway station and steamer pier at Wemyss Bay, opened in 1903, is a fine example of their 'joined-up thinking'.

In the south-west, the Great Western Railway operated services between Weymouth, the Channel Islands and France, while

below: A postcard by Valentines of Dundee. The lower image showing Eastbourne Station was also available as a separate card. The locomotive heading the train is a London, Brighton & South Coast Railway B4 class 4-4-0, designed by R. J. Billinton and built at either Brighton Works between 1899 and 1902, or Sharp, Stewart & Company in Glasgow in 1901.

Eastbourne Express

21

top right: Charing Cross Hotel and Station, London c.1904.

The South Eastern Railway opened the station in January 1864. The Renaissance-style Charing Cross Hotel, designed by Edward Middleton Barry, was opened in May 1865. Barry also designed the Eleanor Cross which stands in front of the hotel, based on the design of a thiteenth century cross which once stood in Whitehall. The station originally had six platforms, roofed with an elegant wrought-iron and glass structure, but part of this roof collapsed in 1905 due to a faulty joint. The South Eastern & Chatham Railway Joint Management Committee – which had been formed in 1899 to operate both the South Eastern Railway and the London, Chatham & Dover Railway elected to replace it rather than attempt the necessary repairs. In so doing, they replaced the elegant with the utilitarian.

right: Horse buses, motor buses, taxis and carriages outside London Victoria Station, terminus of the London, Brighton & South Coast Railway.

from 1898, the South Eastern & Chatham Railway had large steamers sailing out of Dover as part of a through service linking London with Paris. There were many others and, of course, their ships were all featured on series of postcards avidly bought by collectors.

Some aspects of the golden age of the picture postcard did not last long. The increasing popularity of illustrated newspapers and magazines took away a significant part of the market. News cards and disaster cards, and postcards commemorating special events were soon of much more limited commercial value, replaced – and regularly beaten to

the marketplace – by the greater immediacy of the illustrated press. The onset of war also impacted on that market. After peace returned, the range of cards never again achieved the variety available to the Edwardians.

While enthusiasts still bought railway and shipping cards for their collections, the average person sent messages on a somewhat more restricted, and often less engaging, range of views.

The cards selected for this book stretch the definition of the 'Edwardian' era to include the years up to the middle of the 1914-18 war, as that marked an important contraction in sales – a contraction from which the market only partially recovered after hostilities had ceased.

Despite having collected these beautiful cards for more than forty years, I have barely scratched the surface of the huge legacy of railway views which were produced between 1900 and the early years of the Great War.

While the author's name gets prominence on the cover, a book like this depends on input from a great many people, so my sincere thanks are due to the friends and fellow collectors who have drawn my attention to interesting cards, loaned me cards from their collections, or have added to the story with interesting snippets of historical information. They have all enriched this volume.

Thanks also – as ever – to my wife Kath for her constant tolerance and support.

John Hannavy 2017

below: In addition to views of their current operations, the London & North Western Railway published series of cards based on photographs of historic locomotives. This Bloomer Class 2-2-2 *President* was built at Wolverton in 1861.

THE EAST & SOUTH-EAST

IN 2016, LONDON'S WATERLOO STATION was reportedly used by more than 99,000,000 passengers. Euston, in the same period, had a mere forty-two million, while the small station in Shippea Hill, Cambridgeshire, was used by just eighteen – that's not 18,000,000, just 18, and at least two of those were newspaper reporters sent to investigate the place the day after the statistics had been published.

Once a busy goods station with several trains a day transporting locally grown fruit and vegetables to market – and porterage staff to handle it all – Shippea Hill Station had fallen victim to the rise of road transport. The itinerant workforce who harvested the crops had, of course, almost all made their way there by train.

Railway travel was, of course, the marvel of the Victorian age – that same age which oversaw the growth of tourism. Mid-nineteenth century tourist guides foresaw the travel revolution which railways would bring about.

The anonymous writer who wrote one of the earliest guides to the Lake District – *Sylvan's Pictorial Handbook to the English Lakes* published in 1847 – marvelled that 'when it is

top: Waterloo Station was opened in 1848 by the London & South Western Railway. By 1899 it had 16 platforms across three adjacent stations — the original known as Central, flanked by Khartoum and Cyprus. A complete rebuild started in 1904, and by the time this postcard was published, much of the work had been completed.

middle: An early postcard, c.1903, from the Locomotive Publishing Company, based on an 1869 photograph of the Great Northern Railway's Highgate Station.

bottom: The archway — more accurately a Doric 'Propylaeum' — which marked the Drummond Street entrance to Euston Station was designed by Philip Hardwick, completed in 1837, and destroyed in 1962.

left: Paddington Station opened as the terminus of Brunel's broad gauge network in 1854, replacing the Great Western Railway's first central London station which had opened in 1838. The last broad-gauge service left Paddington Station on Friday, 20 May 1892, and the terminus was substantially enlarged between 1906 and 1915.

below left: St Pancras Station was opened by the Midland Railway in 1868, adjacent to the Great Northern Railway's London terminus at King's Cross which had opened in 1852.

Midland Railway, St. Pancras Station.

generally known that in about twelve hours the Tourist may be set down at Kendal, direct from London – at the very gate as it may be termed, of a district universally admitted to be the most beautiful in England – it is not too much to assert that the number of Tourists will annually increase.'

Six decades after 'Sylvan' wrote those words, there would be picture postcards available on the news-stands on just about every station platform along the entire route north.

By the time the second edition of *Baedeker's Guide to Great Britain* was published in 1890, London was the well-

L. B. and N. C. R.   Epsom Downs Station.

above: The photograph used on this postcard is beleved to have been taken on Derby Day 1907 – hence the large number of race day trains. The station, built for the London, Brighton & South Coast Railway – surely the identification on the card is a misprint – was opened in 1865, closed in 1989 and later demolished.

Willesðen Junction

The Wrench Series Nr. 4500

right: The London & North Western Railway's Willesden Junction originally became operational in 1866.

established starting point for foreign visitors – especially Americans – wishing to explore Britain.

The network of railways radiating out from the capital offered relatively easy access to just about everywhere in the country. It was not, of course, the usual point of arrival for American visitors to Britain, as most transatlantic shipping lines plied routes between New York, Boston and Liverpool.

G. E. R. EXPRESS TRAIN.   COLCHESTER STATION

left: Colchester's first station was built by the Eastern Counties Railway and opened in 1843. The ECR had been absorbed into the Great Eastern Railway by 1862.

below: This view of Dugald Drummond-designed 4-4-0 Class L12 locomotive No.421, hauling a Portsmouth train somewhere near Surbiton in Surrey, was published as a postcard by the Locomotive Publishing Company, the photograph probably having been taken when the locomotive was brand new in 1905. On 1 July 1906, No. 421 was one of two locomotives at the head of the Portsmouth to Waterloo mail train which was derailed at Salisbury Station in Wiltshire, killing twenty-eight people and injuring eleven. It had reportedly taken a bend at too high a speed. *The wreckage is illustrated on page 19.*

Train services from Liverpool to London, therefore, were explained in detail.

The book's author – formally referred to in the Preface as 'Mr. J. F. Muirhead, M.A.' – had, it was claimed, 'personally visited the greater part of the districts described', although he acknowledged the input from many local sources.

Scotland, he admitted, was not covered in the same depth as England and Wales, a shortcoming he hoped to rectify in future. He never did.

There are many statistics included in the book which underline the huge importance of the railways at a time when

9255 Pangbourne Station, Berks.

above: Brighton Station was opened in 1840 by the London & Brighton Railway, linking the south coast town to Shoreham-by-Sea along the coast, and later connecting it to London Bridge. The route was engineered by John Urpeth Rastrick — also involved in the design of the station — and based on a proposal by Robert Stephenson, the only son of railway pioneer George Stephenson.

right: Pangbourne Station in Berkshire was opened in 1840 as part of the original section of the Great Western Railway.

the country's population was around 38 million. Muirhead listed the ten largest railway companies by passenger numbers – most of them with a London presence – the largest being the Great Eastern Railway with 73,654,253 passengers.

Of the others with established London termini, the London & North Western Railway, which carried just shy of

60 million, was a long way behind in second place, with the Great Western's 55 million in third place.

None of these, however, was the busiest, that being the London, Chatham & Dover Railway – the smallest network of those cited in *Baedeker* – on whose mere 194 miles of track, more than 28 million passengers were travelling annually, many of them in and out of London Bridge station, then one of the capital's busiest.

above: Purists will recognise that the 1899-1901-built LB&SCR B4 Class locomotive designed by Robert Billinton, seen here in Brighton Station, would have carried the railway's umber livery rather than black.

below left: Mitcham Junction Station, opened in 1868, marked the intersection of the lines operated by the Wimbledon and Croydon Railway (established in 1855) and the London, Brighton & South Coast Railway. The Wimbledon and Croydon Railway trackbed has, since 2000, been part of the Croydon Tramlink network.

right: From around 1905, the L&NWR operated single-car railmotors on lines around Oxford and Cambridge where traffic volume did not warrant a larger train. They were driven by a steam engine at one end of the carriage, exhausting through the roof.

L.& N.W. RAIL MOTOR CAR.—RUNNING ON THE OXFORD & CAMBRIDGE BRANCHES

middle: Some of the 1851 buildings at Etchingham Station seen in this postcard c.1910 still stand. The station is on the line from Charing Cross to Hastings, opened by the South Eastern Railway.

below: A train approaching Hayward's Heath Station, Sussex, c.1905.

Hastings Express running through Etchingham at 60 miles an hour.

ETCHINGHAM

Haywards Heath

By comparison, the London, Brighton & South Coast Railway's 40 million passengers were carried along 476 miles of track. By the dawn of the Edwardian period featured in this book, all those passenger numbers had probably increased, although detailed figures are hard to unravel.

Baedeker's Guide offered its readers some interesting statistics, one of which was the fact that 'In proportion to area and population, the railway-system of Great Britain is more

above: Cambridge Station was opened in 1845 by the Eastern Counties Railway which, by 1862 had been absorbed into the Great Eastern Railway. Standing at the platform in this postcard c.1905 is a James Hudson-designed GER Class S46 4-4-0, built at the company's Stratford Works in London. The station had been extended in 1896 and would be largely rebuilt in 1908.

left: Hackney carriages await passengers outside the London and South Western Railway's Wimbledon Station in this postcard c.1910.

ACCEPTING A TRAIN AT HARROW.
L & N.W. RAILWAY.

extensive than that of any other country in Europe, Belgium excepted', before going on to explain that London alone had more than two hundred stations, including those on the Underground.

At the time Muirhead was compiling his guide, Euston Station was officially known as Euston Square, a name it retained until 1909 when it adopted the shorter name. At the same time, Gower Street Station on the Metropolitan Line – which had been opened in 1863 – changed its name to Euston Square.

In total, *Baedeker* listed no fewer than fourteen London railway termini, drawing attention to the extent and duplication of services and routes – '1. *Euston Square Station*, near Euston Road and

Merton Park. - The Footbridge.

opposite top: A new Harrow-bound Metropolitan Line electric train c.1910. The line was partially electrified by 1906 but initially only as far as Harrow, north of which steam took over. The first 20 locomotives — built between 1904 and 1906 by British Westinghouse at their Trafford Park works in Manchester — were each powered by four 215 hp electric motors

opposite bottom: Harrow signal box, one of the many 'official' cards published by the London & North Western Railway in 1905.

above left: To go to the effort and expense of producing a finely tinted postcard view of a footbridge may seem odd to us today, but it attests to the immense popularity of sending and collecting railway postcards.

RAILWAY STATION
GILLINGHAM KENT

Tottenham Court Road, for the trains of the London & North Western Railway to Rugby, Chester, N. Wales, Holyhead (for Ireland), Birmingham, Liverpool, Manchester, Carlisle, and Scotland. 2. *St Pancras Station*, Euston Road, for the trains of the Midland Railway to Bedford, Derby, Nottingham, Leeds, Manchester, Liverpool, Newcastle, and Scotland. 3. *King's Cross Station*, Euston Road, adjoining the last, for the trains of the Great Northern Co. to Peterborough, Sheffield, York, Hull, Lincoln, Manchester, Liverpool, Newcastle, and Scotland. 4. *Paddington Station*, for the trains of the Great Western Railway to the West and South-West of England, Windsor, Oxford,

left: Gillingham Station in Kent was opened in 1858 as New Brompton Station on the London, Chatham & Dover Railway's main line between Chatham and London Victoria. The station was re-named Gillingham in 1912.

35

top: The Greathead Shield, named after its inventor James Henry Greathead, was used to cut the route of the Great Northern, Piccadilly & Brompton Railway which opened for passengers in December 1906, linking Finsbury Park and Hammersmith. The 14 kilometre (8.8 mile) route, operated by the The Underground Electric Railways Company of London, served 22 stations. An abandoned Greathead Shield reportedly still lies entombed in a disused tunnel close to Moorgate Station.

middle: On the Central London Railway between Shepherd's Bush and Bank, c.1904. 'The Twopenny Tube' — was extended west to Wood Lane in 1908, and east to Liverpool Street in 1912. It is now part of the Central Line.

right: Ealing Broadway Station was first opened as Ealing Station by the Great Western Railway on their broad gauge line between Paddington and Taplow in 1839. It assumed the Ealing Broadway name in 1875. The Victorian platform canopy seen in this c.1908 postcard was demolished in 1961.

EALING BROADWAY STATION (G.W.R.)

GODALMING RAILWAY STATION.

left: Godalming Station, seen here on a postcard c.1910, was opened in 1859 on the route between London Waterloo and Portsmouth. It was originally served by trains from both the London & South Western Railway and the London, Brighton & South Coast Railway.

below: The station at Paddock Wood, originally known as Maidstone Road despite its distance from Maidstone, was opened in 1842 by the South Eastern Railway on the line from Redhill to Dover. It was immortalised by Charles Dickens as the scene of a fictional fatal accident in the novel *Dombey and Son*, when James Carker fell under the wheels of an approaching train. This card was published by Maidstone photographer G. A. Cooper

Birmingham, Liverpool, Manchester, and Wales. 5. *Victoria Station*, Victoria Street, S.W., a double station for the trains of the London, Chatham, and Dover Railway, the London, Brighton, and South Coast Railway, and various suburban lines. 6. *Waterloo Station*, Waterloo Road, for the trains of the London and South-Western Railway to Reading, Windsor, and the South-West of England. 7. *London Bridge Station*, for the Brighton and South Coast Railway. 8. *Charing Cross Station,* close to Trafalgar Square, for the trains of the South Eastern Railway to Tunbridge, Canterbury, Folkestone, Dover, etc., and of local lines. 9. *Cannon Street Station*, the City

THE STATION PADDOCK WOOD

right: A load of Kent hops on a London & North Western Railway cart for transportation to a brewery after being delivered to London Broad Street Station in 1905.

middle: Robert Stephenson's *Invicta* was built in Newcastle for the Canterbury & Whitstable Railway and hauled the first train into Whitstable Harbour Station on 3 May 1830. It was withdrawn from service just eight years later. For many years the locomotive was displayed in Dane John Gardens in Canterbury, but is currently the subject of a restoration project with a view to displaying it in a planned new museum in Whitstable. This Léon & Lévy postcard dates from around 1906.

right: Camden Goods depot opened in 1851. Within a decade it was the main freight station for the North London Railway, which was absorbed into the London & North Western Railway in 1921. This postcard is titled 'A Load of Manchester Goods'.

12 CANTERBURY. — The Invicta 1830. — LL.

BRENTWOOD. — THE STATION.

top: A very quiet day at Hertford Station, as seen in a postcard c.1906. The station was opened by the Great Eastern Railway in February 1888, replacing an earlier one built in 1843 by the 5-foot gauge Northern & Eastern Railway as the terminus of their branch-line from Broxbourne to Hertford. The line had, within a year, become a subsidiary of the Eastern Counties Railway and relaid to standard gauge before becoming part of the GER in 1862. Since 1923 it has been known as Hertford East.

left: When this card was published c.1910, Brentwood Station was known as Brentwood & Warley, its name since 1889. It had been opened in 1840 by the Eastern Counties Railway on their route from Liverpool Street. By 1843, the line had been extended to Colchester, becoming part of the GER in 1862. In November 1902, 80 passengers were injured when a goods train collided with the rear of an Ipswich to Liverpool Street passenger train waiting at the station. The goods train's driver was deemed responsible.

terminus for the same lines as Charing Cross. 10. *Ludgate Hill*, and 11. *Holborn Viaduct*, City termini of the London, Chatham, and Dover Railway, and of local lines. 12. *Liverpool Street Station*, for the trains of the Great Eastern Railway to Cambridge, Lincoln, the Eastern Counties, and local stations. 13. *Broad Street Station*, adjoining the last, for the local trains of the North London Railway. 15. *Fenchurch Street Station*, near the Bank, for Blackwall, Gravesend, Southend, etc.' Due to a typographical error, there was no No.14 on the list.

By the time the 1900 edition of *Baedeker's Guide to London and its Environs* was published, the number of major stations had been increased to 17 with the addition of Marylebone

right & middle:
A signalling error
caused the
Sharnbrook train
crash in Bedfordshire
on 4 February 1909
when a fast Midland
Railway goods train
from Manchester to
London ploughed into
a stationary goods
train, killing the
driver and fireman of
the Manchester train.
The top postcard
comes from a series
produced by a local
photographer, while
the middle card was
published by Warner
Gothard of Barnsley,
using photographs
taken by S. Percival
of Kettering.

bottom: The train
crash at Ilford on
1 January 1915 holds
the dubious record
of being the railway
accident which
resulted in the
highest number of
people being injured.
Ten were killed, but
the number hurt
exceeded 500 when
a Great Eastern
Railway express train
from Clacton-on-Sea
to London Liverpool
Street passed two
danger signals and
collided with a local
train which was
crossing over from
one line to another
just to the west of
the station.

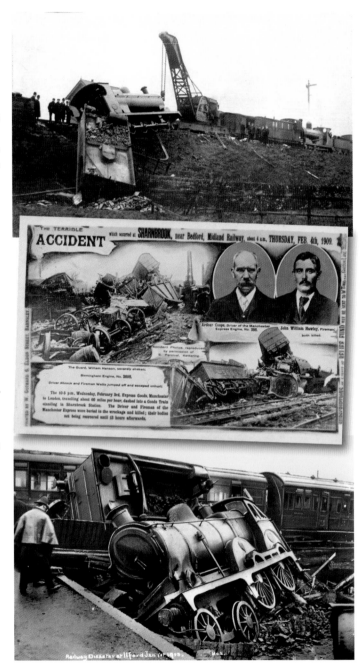

Mishap to Large Goods Train Engine at Tunbridge Wells Station, March 11th., 1905.

top: The Witham train crash happened on 1 September 1905 when all fourteen coaches on the Great Eastern Railway's express train from London Liverpool Street to Cromer came off the rails at Witham between Chelmsford and Colchester as the train sped through the Essex station. Ten passengers and a porter were killed, with seventy passengers injured, much of the station being destroyed in the accident.

middle: Warner Gothard's postcard of the Tonbridge Junction train crash on 5 March 1909 marked the first of three fatal railway accidents in 1909 — the others being at Cardiff in April and West Hampstead in October. The crash occurred when a train to Redhill overran a signal and collided with the mail and boat train from Charing Cross to Dover. The fireman and an inspector were killed and 11 passengers injured.

left: A goods engine derailed in the turntable pit at Tunbridge Wells Station, 11 March 1905, photographed and published as a postcard by Lankester & Co.

right: The London, Tilbury & Southend Railway opened Westcliff-on-Sea Station in 1895, the penultimate station on the line to Southend. This postcard dates from c.1910. The station's name was shortened to 'Westcliff' in 1969.

middle: Ramsgate Harbour Station was separated from the beach only by a low wall. It was opened in 1863 as Ramsgate, the terminus of the Kent Coast Railway's extension from Herne Bay. In 1873 the KCR became part of the London, Chatham & Dover Railway and the station's name was changed to Ramsgate & St Lawrence-on-Sea, before changing again in 1899 to Ramsgate Harbour. It closed in 1926.

bottom: The station at Barcombe in East Sussex was opened as New Barcombe by the London, Brighton & South Coast Railway in 1882 on the Lewes to East Grinstead line. The line was closed to passenger traffic in 1955 and the station is now a private house. Part of the line is now celebrated as the Bluebell Railway, but Barcombe is not part of that.

THE EAST & SOUTH-EAST

THEYDON BOIS: STATION.

left: For its first few months in 1845, Theydon Bois Station was known simply as Theydon. It was opened by the Great Eastern Railway. Today it is penultimate station on the TfL Central Line route from Stratford to Epping. The locomotive is believed to be a GER Class C32 designed by James Holden in the early 1890s, and built at Stratford.

(opened in 1898), Baker Street, and St Pauls, and the total number of stations had risen to 300.

Baedeker told his readers that the cost of building the Metropolitan Railway had been £1M a mile – a phenomenal amount of money in the second half of the nineteenth century – and that the underground network was, by 1900, carrying more than 150 million passengers per year in three classes of carriages. By comparison, more than a century later – and with class distinction a thing of the distant past – the latest figures available from Transport for London (TfL) put annual passenger journeys on the tube system at 1.34 billion.

below: Kent House Station in Beckenham was opened by the London, Chatham & Dover Railway in 1884. At the platform in this c.1905 postcard is a South Eastern & Chatham Railway train en route from London Victoria to Orpington. The locomotive appears to be an A1 Class 0-4-4T locomotive, designed for the LC&DR by William Kirtley and built in the 1870s by Kitson & Company in Leeds. However the number '700' does not appear in lists of the numbers allocated to this class of locomotive.

Kent House Station.

right: Now the site of a caravan park, Slinfold Station was opened in 1865 by the London, Brighton & South Coast Railway on a single track branch-line between Guildford and Horsham. The tank engine in this 1907 card by H. Homewood of Burgess Hill, is a Robert Billinton-designed LB&SCR E5 Class 0-6-2T built at Brighton 1902-04.

below: Eastbourne Station was rebuilt in 1886 by the LB&SCR. The locomotive heading the train out of the station in this c.1906 view appears to be a B2 Class 4-4-0, another Billinton design.

Most of the railway companies were happy to welcome the postcard companies' photographers, and by 1904-5 postcards were available, monochrome or tinted, of most of the stations and their trains. Many of the rural stations celebrated in those coloured cards were unlikely to have warranted such investment by the publishers, passenger numbers unlikely to have ever offered sufficient sales.

Slinfold Station, L. B. & S. C. Ry. Sussex.

Eastbourne Station

G. E. R. Four Coupled Passenger Engine. No. 486.

left: Great Eastern Railway No.486, one of the GER's T26 Class 2-4-0 locomotives, designed by James Holden and built at the Stratford Works between 1891 and 1894. The postcard was No.54 in a Locomotive Publishing Company series printed in Berlin and published c.1904. The locomotives were regularly used on routes into Norfolk and Suffolk. One example, the 1894-built No.490, is preserved in the National Railway Museum in York.

It is a sad reflection of today's utilitarian approach to railway infrastructure, that many of the small stations celebrated on postcards a century ago have had their fine Victorian and Edwardian buildings replaced by glorified bus shelters. The Edwardian romance of the railways is now as long-forgotten as the dreams of wealth which motivated their Victorian investors.

Many more, of course, have disappeared altogether in the name of cost efficiency – some having suffered the ultimate in ignominious ends by being covered over in tarmac and re-used as parking sites for the cars which brought about their demise.

below: Berwick Station in Sussex was planned by the London & Brighton Railway, but by the time it opened in 1846, the L&BR had become part of the newly-formed London, Dover & South Coast Railway. It was a stop on their route from London Victoria to Eastbourne.

Berwick Station, looking East, L. B. & S. C. Ry.

THE SOUTH & SOUTH-WEST

GOD'S WONDERFUL RAILWAY, THE GWR, has long been synonymous with the south and south-west of England. Originally engineered by Isambard Kingdom Brunel, the Great Western Railway was conceived as a high-speed broad-gauge railway linking London with Bristol. With the acquisition of the Bristol & Exeter Railway in January 1876 its network extended to the far south-west. GWR routes also went north into the Midlands, and into South Wales.

It was also referred to as the 'Great Way Round' thanks to its many holiday destinations, but on bad days in more recent privatised and franchised times, 'Goes Wrong Regularly' has also been somewhat cruelly suggested.

Swindon, approximately half way between London and Bristol, was chosen as the site of Brunel's locomotive works, and it is said that the first buildings on the site were faced with stone excavated during the digging of Box Tunnel.

The original GWR line was soon fed by countless small independent branch-lines, but by the dawn of the postcard era, it had swallowed most of them up.

opposite: Detail from a postcard c.1903. This level crossing in Copnor Road, Portsmouth, featured in several early postcards until replaced by a railway bridge in 1908. This 'Trichromatic Series' postcard was produced by well-known Portsmouth publishers J. Welch & Sons and, according to the legend on the back 'Printed at our Works in Belgium'.

below: Dinner time at the GWR Swindon Works c.1905, with workers and apprentices posing for the camera.

right: The GWR's Swindon Junction Station was opened in 1842, and became the junction of the railway's three main lines to Bristol, South Wales and Gloucester. It was sited close to the locomotive and engineering works. The wide gap between tracks seen on this postcard c.1907 is a legacy of its broad-gauge days. In Victorian times, most trains made extended stops at Swindon to change locomotives, but that practice was discontinued in 1895. The station was demolished in the early 1970s when the area was redeveloped.

G. W. R. Station, Swindon

right: This George Jackson Churchward-designed 2-6-2T locomotive freshly outshopped from the Swindon Works in 1903, was the fore-runner of many GWR tank engine designs. It was extensively tested for over a year before any more were built. Later designated as the first of the 3100 Class, the design was successively adapted by both Churchward and later Charles Collett. The first of the 'Large Prairie' class of locomotives, 40 of which were eventually built.

G. W. R. New Suburban Tank Locomotive

As the nineteenth century drew to a close, the Swindon Works probably employed around three-quarters of the town's workforce, building new locomotives and rolling stock. From 1892 when the broad gauge era came to an end, converting as many of the two hundred engines originally built to run on Brunel's 7ft. gauge as could economically be re-used on the 4ft.8½ins. standard gauge which had been adopted across the rest of the railway system.

Changing from broad gauge to standard gauge was a monumental undertaking, yet the changeover was completed with remarkably little interruption to services. Meticulously

F. G. O. Stuart, 704. L. & S. W. Ry Works, Eastleigh.

left: The London
& South Western
Railway's locomotive
works at Eastleigh,
from a postcard
produced by
Southampton-based
publishers
F.G.O.Stuart c.1904.
The works had
opened as a carriage
works in 1891, being
expanded to include
locomotive-building
after the promotion
of Ardrossan-born
Dugald Drummond
to Chief Mechanical
Engineer in 1905.

planned, and undertaken over a period of years from the
1870s – including a period when several lines operated as
dual-gauge – the last broad-gauge train ran on Friday 20 May
1892 between Exeter and Penzance. That was followed by the
conversion of the final 177 miles of track – mainline and
branch-lines along that same route – to standard gauge over
just a single weekend – a lesson there to be learned by
Network Rail.

below: The Swindon,
Marlborough &
Andover Railway's
Swindon Town
Station, opened in
1881, joined the
Midland & South
Western Junction
Railway's network
in 1884. Passenger
services were
withdrawn in 1961.

M. and S.W.R. Station, Old Swindon

right: Camborne Station in Cornwall, as it looked around 1906, just after the station had been rebuilt in GWR style. Originally opened as a broad gauge branch line by the Hayle Railway in 1837, it became part of the West Cornwall Railway in 1846. Although the WCR remained nominally independent until nationalised, the route was jointly operated for many years by the Great Western, the Somerset & Dorset and the Bristol & Exeter Railway, all three of which were also originally broad gauge

Camborne Station

The broad-gauge locomotives and rolling stock still in service were all taken back to Swindon where, over the following years, parts from a large proportion of them were salvaged and, where practicable, re-used.

Swindon Works enjoyed an extended heyday from the Victorian era right through to the outbreak of the Second World War, but after nationalisation work declined, the site eventually being closed in 1986. Today, the historic buildings house the Great Western Steam Museum, the headquarters of both English Heritage and the National Trust, and a large retail shopping outlet.

below: Fratton Station near Portsmouth was opened in 1885 and was served by both the London, Brighton & South Coast Railway and the London & South Western. The line on which it stands had been planned by the Brighton & Chichester Railway in 1844, but by the time it was opened to Fratton and Portsmouth in 1847 it had been absorbed into the LB&SCR.

Fratton Railway Station

The Railway Station, St. Ives

The region's other great locomotive works – the London & South Western Railway's works at Eastleigh in Hampshire – continues as a carriage repair facility to this day, with a large part of the works now used as a railway store.

By the early years of the twentieth century, while the mainline railway network was experiencing heavy usage, the economics of running locomotive-hauled trains along the

above: A busy scene at St Ives Station, photographed c. 1910. The twin-track broad gauge branch line which terminated at St Ives had been opened by the GWR in 1877, being converted to standard gauge over a weekend in May 1892. The station seen here was closed in 1971 and the town is now served by a single platform in the former goods yard.

left: Other cards may have been sold at Studley Station in Gloucestershire, originally opened by the Evesham & Redditch Railway in 1868, but the footbridge is an odd choice.

Lower Studley.

top: Devonport Station, between Plymouth and Plymouth Dockyard, was opened by the Cornwall Railway in 1859 and taken over by the Great Western in 1889

middle: An unusual configuration of vehicles heading towards Brunel's single track Royal Albert Bridge across the River Tamar at Saltash, seen here in a 1905 postcard. Nearest the camera is a railmotor pushing a driving trailer with, in front of both of them, what appears to be a small tank engine and another driving trailer. Working such a combination would have required the close co-ordination of both crews. The Royal Albert Bridge had been opened by Prince Albert in 1859.

bottom: A railmotor and driving trailer at Warren Halt near Dawlish in 1906, one of several 'halts' opened in 1905 by the GWR after the introduction of railmotors. It was such a success that the platform was doubled in length in 1906 to facilitate longer trains. By 1911 it was upgraded to a station, renamed Dawlish Warren. A completely rebuilt station opened in 1912.

L. & S. W. Railway Station   Devonport.

Royal Albert Bridge from the Station.   Saltash.

The Warren Halt, Dawlish.

hundreds of miles of rural lines was already being questioned. There were simply just not enough passengers to make the operation of even relatively short trains commercially viable.

In addressing that challenge, the London & South Western Railway was the first company to look at the concept of the railmotor – a self-contained steam-powered single vehicle with open-plan seating.

above: Newquay Station, seen here in a postcard, published c.1908, was built in 1905 at the terminus of a former mineral railway by the Great Western who had been running passenger trains into the town since 1876, buying out the mineral company in 1877. The line to Truro was a casualty of the Beeching cuts, and today the station has just a single platform.

left: Newton Abbot Station was opened in 1846 by the South Devon Railway, which merged with the GWR in 1876. The line remained broad gauge until 1892.

top: A 1904 Swindon-built GWR railmotor with driving trailer behind, at Saltash Station c.1908.

bottom: Devizes Station was another casualty of closures. Built on a branch line by the Wiltshire, Somerset & Weymouth Railway, it opened in 1857, closing 109 years later. Since 1966, the large market town has had no railway connection at all. Although legally an independent operation, the WS&WR was backed by the GWR and the track was originally laid to Brunel's broad gauge specification.

Motor Train
Saltash Station

The GWR saw the potential of such vehicles, and actually borrowed two from the L&SWR to evaluate their capabilities, resulting in the decision to design and build their own variant, the first of which entered service in 1903. Designed by George Churchward, the majority were built at Swindon, and by 1908, when the last was rolled out, the fleet numbered 99 units.

The steam engine powered a four-coupled bogey at one end of the vehicle. While they were cheaper to operate than conventional locomotive-hauled trains, they were difficult to maintain – the GWR built an extra dozen or so interchangeable vertical-boilered steam engines for the 99

G. W. Ry Station. Devizes.

CENTRAL STATION BOURNEMOUTH

Three of the many postcard views of Bournemouth Central Station, published between 1904 and 1910.

top: Passengers boarding a steam railmotor c.1910.

middle: Joseph Welch & Sons' cards were published as 'JWS Series'. Based at Mile End, Portsmouth, they published a large series of cards from 1903 onwards.

bottom: Lévy, Sons & Co. were based in Paris and London. Their cards carried the monogram 'L.L.' from their original name of Léon & Lévy. This view is dated c.1905.

Central Railway Station, Bournemouth.

72 BOURNEMOUTH. — The Central Station. — Interior. — LL.

55

top: The Helston Railway Company opened its line to Helston in Cornwall in 1887, but by 1898 the company had been absorbed into the Great Western Railway. This postcard of Helston Station was photographed and published as a postcard c.1907 by E. & E. Bragg of Redruth. The photograph was taken by Edward Albert Bragg, 1877-1928, a well-known professional photographer and chronicler of Cornish life.

right: Outside Helston Station, just about every sort of transport awaited Edwardian visitors — a motor charabanc, a GWR motor bus, an express stagecoach and a carriage. The bus was one of the first batch of 16hp Milnes-Daimler single-deck buses acquired by the GWR in 1903, and operated on a route to Penzance and the Lizard.

Helston, Motor Cars leaving for Lizard.

railmotors to minimise the time each unit would be out of service. They were also difficult to keep clean with just a simple partition separating the passenger accommodation from the steam engine at one end of the 70ft (31 metre) coach.

When the vehicle was running with the steam engine end leading, driver and fireman worked together in the cab – known as the 'vestibule' – but for the return journey, they were at opposite ends, their only communication being a series of coded bell signals.

With the introduction of the railmotor came un-manned station halts, with the guard issuing tickets and giving passengers the same sort of 'hop on, hop off' freedom they had with trams and buses. Several such halts were built around Gloucester and on the GWR's South Devon routes.

The railmotor's popularity led to another innovation – as passenger numbers increased the capacity of a single vehicle proved insufficient, and that was doubled by coupling it to a driving trailer, enabling 2-car push-pull operation.

This first use of 'multiple units' presaged the DMUs and EMUs we have to put up with to today. However, as there were only mechanical linkages between the engine and the remote driving position, they were physically demanding on the driver who had to exert a great deal of effort to control the engine via 140ft-long steel connecting rods.

below left: Bratton Fleming Station on the Lynton & Barnstaple Railway, a narrow-gauge line which ran across Exmoor in Devon. The railway opened to traffic in 1898 and was closed in 1935. For the past thirty years, a local enthusiasts' group has been working towards re-opening the full 19 mile line. The station building is now a private house.

bottom: A Manning Wardle 2-6-2T locomotive and train prepare to depart from Lynton Station, the terminus of the Lynton & Barnstaple Railway, seen here in a Stengel postcard c.1910.

Lynton and Barnstaple Railway. Bratton Fleming Station.

Lynton Station.

top: The wide gap between the up and down tracks at Tilehurst Station near Reading recalls the line's early broad-gauge days. Although the line was opened by the GWR in 1841, the station dates from forty years later.

middle: Once the terminus of the GWR line from Chippenham, Westbury Station — as seen here in a postcard c.1908 — had been completely rebuilt and enlarged in 1899 when it became a key junction. It remains a busy station today on the Bristol to Paddington line.

bottom: The Midland Railway's terminus in Bath was originally opened as Queen Square Station in 1870. From 1874 it was used by both the Midland and the Somerset & Dorset Joint Railway. Under British Railways the station's name was changed to Bath Green Park, which it retained until closure in 1966. Today the Grade II* listed building is used as a covered market and events space.

Tilehurst Station near Reading.

G.W.R. Westbury

80 BATH. — Midland Railway Station. — LL.

left: Topsham
Station, despite its
grand appearance,
was a stop on a
branch-line between
Exmouth and Exeter
in Devon. Opened by
the London & South
Western Railway in
1861 it also served as
a passing place on an
otherwise single
track line.

below: One of
the many stations
on the Great Western
line to have
been abandoned,
Lavington Station in
Littleton Pannell was
opened by the GWR
in 1900 on their Stert
& Westbury line,
a few miles from
Devizes, Wiltshire.
After the closure of
Devizes Station in
1966, it was the
closest station to
the Wiltshire town
until it too was
closed in 1979.

Another disadvantage was their limited power, which proved inadequate even on moderate gradients, and many railmotors later had their steam engines removed and were used as auto-trailers coupled to a conventional locomotive.

Today, of course, many of the branch-lines on which these vehicles ran are long gone, victims of railway rationalisation and the unstoppable advance of the motor car.

Two of the last batch of vehicles, built at Swindon in 1908, have been lovingly restored – No.93 as a railmotor, No.92 as an auto-trailer – and despite being wooden-bodied they are cleared for main line running, and can be seen working on heritage railways and occasionally on selected main lines.

THE MIDLANDS

IN THE HEYDAY OF THE EDWARDIAN RAILWAYS, workers trains were notoriously basic – seldom more clearly evidenced than in the postcard, *below*, of Derbyshire miners making their way home from work in an open Midland Railway coal wagon. The lucky few enjoyed the 'comfort' of sitting on wooden bench seats in a pair of four-wheeled third class carriages, but for many – all of whom were presumably paying for the journey – there was no protection whatsoever from the elements.

Had there been an accident, however, their fate might have been no more serious than their colleagues in the coaches, as these notoriously flimsy wooden-bodied vehicles crumpled into matchwood in the event of a derailment.

Long before the end of the Victorian era, the Midland Railway's network had been extended from its Derby headquarters far beyond the geographical Midlands, stretching to Carlisle in the north, Heysham in Lancashire from where their Irish Sea ferries sailed, as far south-west as Swansea, Bristol and Bath, and, of course, to London.

opposite page: Two views of Birmingham New Street Station.

below: Derbyshire miners pose for the camera while riding home from work in coal wagons.

overleaf: Derby Station c.1910. The first station was opened in 1840 by the North Midlands Railway, who soon shared it with the Birmingham & Derby Junction Railway and the Midland Counties Railway. They merged to become the Midland Railway in 1844, the station then being re-named Derby Midland.

DERBYSHIRE MINERS LEAVING WOR

right: Produced by The Locomotive Publishing Company Ltd at 3 Amen Corner, London E.C. in 1905, this gravure-printed card shows the first of the Midland Railway's 1400 Class 2-4-0 locomotives designed by Samuel Waite Johnson, 60 of which were built between 1879 and 1881 — 30 each at the Midland Railway's Derby Works (Nos.1400-1409 and 1472-1491) and by Neilsen & Company at their Hyde Park Works in Springburn, Glasgow (Nos.1502-1531).

middle: The Wenlock, Craven Arms & Lightmoor Extension Railway drew up plans for Coalbrookdale Station in 1861, but by the time it opened, the company had shortened its name to the Wenlock Railway. Always worked by the GWR, the line was absorbed in 1896. The station closed in 1965.

right: Grindleford Station was opened by the Midland Railway in 1894 and stands at the western entrance to the Totley Tunnel on the Sheffield & Midland Railway Company's line to Manchester — now known as the Hope Valley Line.

Coalbrookdale Station

GRINDLEFORD STATION

64

Kirby Muxloe Station.

left: The Midland Railway opened Kirby Muxloe Station — first as a temporary station in 1848, with a permanent station being completed in 1859 — as part of its route from Leicester to Burton-on-Trent which was completed in 1849. An early casualty of the Beeching cuts, the station was closed to passenger traffic in 1964 and, despite several moves to re-open it over the years, it never happened. The line remained open to freight. The most recent proposal was in 2009, and that would have included the building of a new station at Kirby Muxloe, but as yet that has not been translated into action.

In addition to the Midland, across the region the dominant railway companies included the Great Northern Railway, the London & North Western and, of course, the Great Western.

The Midland had been formed in 1844 when three smaller companies were merged – the North Midland Railway, the Midland Counties Railway and the Birmingham & Derby Junction Railway.

By 1867 the Midland had expanded its route network south to London – opening St Pancras Station in 1868 – and north, via the Cheshire Lines Committee network, to Manchester Central Station in 1880.

The first London to Birmingham train service had actually been instigated as early as 1838, running into Curzon Street

below: Built in 1846 by the Bedford Railway — later a constituent company of the London & North Western Railway — Fenny Stratford Station's layout was unusual in that the two platforms did not face each other in the conventional way, but were staggered. The station, as seen in this postcard c.1905 was re-laid in 1948 to a conventional pattern, but by 1960 only one platform was in use and today it is single track.

L. and N.-W. Railway Station, Fenny Stratford

top: A 'Precedent' Class 2-4-0 locomotive stands at the head of a London & North Western Railway train in Rugby Station c.1904. The 'Precedent' Class was introduced in 1875 and, along with the slightly smaller 'Precursor' Class introduced a year earlier, these locomotives were the workhorses of the L&NWR for many years

middle: Stamford East Station in Lincolnshire was opened in 1856 as the terminus of the Stamford & Essendine Railway and closed in 1957, although many of its passenger services had been withdrawn as early as 1929. From 1872, the line was operated by the Great Northern Railway, which officially leased the railway in 1892.

bottom: The cause of the 1906 sleeper and mail train crash at Grantham in Lincolnshire was never discovered. The train should have stopped at the station, but sped past danger signals and through the station at over 40mph and derailed on a sharp bend. Both of the crew on the Waverley to Kings Cross express were amongst the 14 fatalities.

THE TERRIBLE RAILWAY DISASTER AT GRANTHAM.—SEPT. 19th, 1906.
Showing the Scattered Mails.

Station – one of several station buildings across the country to claim to be the world's oldest – part of which still stands a short distance from the present-day site of Birmingham New Street.

Birmingham New Street Station was owned and operated by the London & North Western Railway, and for a time it had the largest single-arched roof in the world measuring 212ft (64.6 metres) wide and 840ft (246 metres) long. With the opening of St Pancras with its massive roof, the New Street canopy was relegated to second place.

below & bottom: Two contrasting views of Acocks Green and South Yardley Station on the GWR's line from Banbury to Birmingham Snow Hill and Wolverhampton. The tinted card shows a GWR local passenger service leaving for Birmingham c.1904 while a team of labourers carry out maintenance work on the track. The wide gap between the lines is a legacy of the GWR's broad-gauge days. The sepia postcard, published a few years later, shows the new station after it was extensively rebuilt in 1906-07, with passengers awaiting the arrival of a Birmingham train.

top: An unusual elevated view of the exterior of the London & North Western Railway's Birmingham New Street Station, from a postcard published in 1906. The original station is on the left, with the curved 1885 extension — largely used by the Midland Railway — on the right.

right: Birmingham Snow Hill Station, fronted by the Great Western Hotel, was opened by the GWR in 1852, after the London & North Western denied it access to Curzon Street Station. Snow Hill had already been extensively rebuilt twice before this postcard was published c.1910, and would be expanded yet again by 1914.

bottom: A series of postcards recorded the arrival of King Edward VII & Queen Alexandra at New Street Station in July 1909. The Royal Visit was for the formal opening of Birmingham University, established in 1900 by Queen Victoria.

Station, Bromyard

left: A busy scene on a usually quiet railway. Bromyard Station was opened in 1877 by the Worcester, Leominster and Bromyard Railway Company. The GWR, who had operated the line since it opened, bought the bankrupt company in 1888. The line west of Bromyard closed in 1952, the remainder in 1964.

below: The Much Wenlock & Severn Junction Railway opened the branch line from Buildwas to Much Wenlock in 1862. The West Midland Railway operated services until the line was taken over by the GWR in 1896.

The L&NWR shared the station with the Midland, thanks to a 'right of access' agreement which predated the Midland's formation, and when the station was expanded in 1885 across to the opposite side of Queen's Drive, the Midland had almost exclusive use of the new part of the building, although some of its services used the established L&NWR platforms and vice versa.

With the opening of the curved extension, New Street became Britain's largest railway station, covering an area of just under 5 hectares, or around 12 acres.

Much Wenlock Station.

right: Longeaton, or Long Eaton Station in Derbyshire, seen in a postcard c.1903. The present station to bear that name is some distance from the one illustrated here. In the early days, some small print run postcards were hand-tinted, as in this example, rather than chromo-lithographed.

middle: A London & North Western Railway 'official' postcard from 1904 showing the gantry signals approaching Rugby Station. The upper and lower set of signals were duplicates, designed to ensure drivers always had a clear view as trains approached. This photograph was taken before 1895.

bottom: Colwick Station was opened in 1850 on the Ambergate, Nottingham, Boston & Eastern Junction Railway which, by 1860 had changed its name to the slightly more manageable Nottingham & Grantham Railway & Canal Company. By then the line had been leased to the Great Northern Railway who operated services along it until it passed to the LNER in 1923. This postcard dates from c.1903.

Milford Station, Stafford

left: A W.H.Smith's Series postcard of Milford Station in Staffordshire, c.1910. Known for a time as Milford and Brocton, the station was opened in 1877 on the Trent Valley line – now part of the West Coast Main Line – between Stafford and Colwich Junction, but it was closed in the 1950s and no trace remains today.

below: The Great Western Railway opened Earlswood Lakes Station in 1908. The line had been built by the Birmingham, North Warwickshire & Stratford-upon-Avon Railway which the GWR had taken over in 1900. The route linked Birmingham Snow Hill with Stratford-upon-Avon. Today it is known simply as Earlswood. This beautifully chromo-lithographed postcard was published when the station was newly opened, hence the pristine condition of platforms and buildings.

While the L&NWR had allowed the Midland access to New Street, it had been much less generous to the Great Western back in the late 1840s – which clearly had plans to move north into L&NWR territory – refusing to allow access to Curzon Street, and prompting the GWR to build its own grand station, fronted by an impressive hotel, at Snow Hill.

By the late 1890s the Midland Railway had swallowed up more than thirty other smaller operations and boasted a network of over 5000 track miles including goods yards.

While Derby, Leicester and Birmingham all became important Midland Railway hubs, Derby was chosen as the

Earlswood Lakes Station.

MIDLAND STATION INTERIOR. NOTTINGHAM.

above: Nottingham's Midland Railway Station was opened in 1848, but the layout seen in this postcard dates from a 1904 rebuild.

right: Typographical errors are clearly not just a modern phenomenon as this 1906 postcard of Sherwood Station near 'Nottihgham' proves. The station was built by the Nottingham Suburban Railway Company and welcomed its first passengers in 1889, but just a decade after this card appeared, the station was closed. From the outset trains were operated by the Great Northern Railway.

SHERWOOD STATION. NOTTINGHAM.

centre for the construction and maintenance of the company's engines and rolling stock.

By the early twentieth century more than 40,000 people were employed in the Midland Railway Locomotive Works and the nearby carriage works, both adjacent to the city's station, building around forty new engines annually for the company.

Railway Station, King's Heath

left: King's Heath Station, Birmingham was opened by the Birmingham & Gloucester Railway in 1840, on a line between Kings Norton and Birmingham New Street. It was closed in 1941. There are plans to re-open the line by 2025, but with trains terminating at Birmingham Moor Street, via a new viaduct, rather than New Street.

Amongst the many vehicles they built in 1904 were two railmotors for use on the Morecambe to Heysham line, one of which – at Heysham Station – is illustrated on page 103.

From 1844, until grouping in 1922, the Midland Railway had just four Chief Mechanical Engineers – the first two, Matthew Kirtley and Samuel W. Johnson, occupying the post for twenty-nine and thirty years respectively. Johnson had railways in his blood, having held similar posts at the Manchester, Sheffield & Lincolnshire Railway, the Edinburgh & Glasgow Railway, and the Great Eastern Railway. His son would later become Superintendent of the Great North of Scotland Railway.

below: Midland Railway Class 1853 4-2-2 locomotive No.1865, designed by Samuel W. Johnson and built at Derby in the early 1890s. A Locomotive Publishing Company postcard from c.1904. Johnson's 4-2-2 express engines evolved over a period of years, the driving wheels increasing from 7ft.4ins. to 7ft.9ins. The Class 1853 locomotives – of which more than forty were built – had 7ft.6ins. driving wheels. One example of a slightly later evolution of the design – the Class 115 – and carrying No.673, is preserved in the National Railway Museum collection.

No. 1865. SINGLE EXPRESS, MIDLAND RAILWAY. *By The Locomotive Publishing Company, Ltd., London, E.C. 249.*

73

YORKSHIRE & THE NORTH-EAST

THE NINETEENTH CENTURY must have been an exciting times in which to live. The rate of industrial progress was increasing exponentially, and the transport systems which have now been taken for granted for a hundred and eighty years were just being developed.

While the railways around Newcastle developed into a complex network, as far as Edwardian postcard publishers were concerned it was the claim that the lattice of tracks outside the city's railway station comprised 'the largest

opposite page: The new electric train sets introduced to Newcastle in 1904 were a magnet for photographers and were featured on numerous postcards. The first route had been inaugurated between Newcastle Central Station and Tynemouth on 29 March 1904 using a 600 volt DC third-rail system.

left: One of the many postcards of the 'largest railway junction in the world' outside Newcastle Central Station.

Largest Railway Crossing in the World, Newcastle.
William Smith, Photographer, Gosport.

below: The old and the new — an electric train passes a steam train just outside the station where the tracks branch either side of Newcastle's mediaeval castle Keep. The railway viaduct carrying the East Coast Main Line runs between the castle's Keep and Gatehouse, a shocking indictment of the disregard Victorian railway engineers showed for the country's architectural heritage.

right: The entrance to Newcastle Central Station, seen from the top of the mediaeval castle.

below: An animated scene in Newcastle Central, dating from around 1906. The station had been opened on 29 August 1850, Queen Victoria arriving by train to carry out the ceremony. Central Station replaced two earlier stations, the York, Newcastle & Berwick Railway's services using it from 30 August, with Newcastle & Carlisle Railway trains being operating out of the new station from 1 January 1851.

railway junction in the world' which sold cards! The trackwork was photographed for several publishers, some cards just showing the empty rails, but others featuring the steam and electric rolling stock of the day.

From Newcastle, a rail link to Carlisle was opened in 1838, lines to Darlington in 1844, north to Berwick-upon-Tweed in 1847, and south to London by the end of that decade.

His Majesty King Edward VII
Opening King Edward Bridge,
Newcastle-on-Tyne, July 10, 1906.

BY SPECIAL PERMISSION, HENDERSON & BIRKETT.

Before that, anyone travelling further than walking distance would have had to use one of the many long-distance coaches which travelled along less than comfortably smooth roads.

Stockton and Darlington are, of course, recognised as the birthplaces of the railway, and the north-east embraced the railway age with great enthusiasm – building many of the

above: The postcard as news medium — the King performing the official opening ceremony for the King Edward VII Bridge over the Tyne. The bridge was designed by Charles A. Harrison, Chief Civil Engineer to the North Eastern Railway, and built by the Cleveland Bridge & Engineering Company.

left: Yarm-on-Tees Station was opened in 1852 by the Leeds Northern Railway between Northallerton and Eaglescliffe. It was closed in 1960 but a new station closer to Yarm was opened in 1996. The old station buildings still stand.

Yarm-on-Tees, Railway Station.   No. 1547.

right: A postcard c.1910 showing the trackwork and signalling outside York Station.

middle & bottom: By the early 1900s, Stephenson's *Locomotion No.1* had already been a museum piece for nearly fifty years. Withdrawn from service in 1841, the locomotive spent some years as a stationary engine before being preserved in 1857 at Alfred Kitching's workshops in Darlington. In 1892 it was put on display on a plinth on one of the platforms at the North Eastern Railway's new Darlington Station — opened that year — alongside Timothy Hackworth's 1845 0-6-0 locomotive *Derwent*, built by W. & A. Kitching for the Stockton & Darlington Railway. There they both remained until 1975, being the subject of many postcards from around 1904. Both locomotives are now part of the National Railway Museum collection, and both are on display at *Head of Steam*, the Darlington Railway Centre and Museum.

York Station.

left: This striking view of the interior of York Station was published by Friths, both in sepia and tinted, in 1910.

below: Valentine of Dundee captured the elegant sweep of the interior of York Station. It was also available either in monochrome or finely tinted. For the tinted version, steam from the departing train has been painted out by the company artist.

great routes which still exist today, but also constructing countless local branch-lines the potential of which to ever make a profit was somewhere firmly in the realms of whimsy. As a result, a lot of investors lost a

Railway Station, York.

York Railway Station

Blßom, Picture P.C. Emporium, York Valentines Series

right: The interior of Leeds New Station, 1906. The station had been opened in 1869 by a consortium of the North Eastern Railway and the London & North Western Railway. It was demolished and rebuilt in 1938.

below right: Holmfirth Station was opened in 1850 by the Liverpool & Manchester Railway, successor to the Huddersfield & Sheffield Junction Railway which had originally planned the route before being taken over in 1847. From the outset, services were actually operated by the Manchester, Sheffield & Lincolnshire Railway before passing to the Lancashire & Yorkshire Railway in 1870. The terminus of a short branch line, it had just a single platform and probably never enjoyed sufficient passenger numbers to justify its existence, let alone the scale of its buildings. It was closed to passengers in 1959, finally closing altogether in 1965.

Leeds New Station (from the East End).

HOLMFIRTH STATION.

lot of money laying tracks which today survive only as footpaths and cycle routes. Others, of course, now form part of the Tyneside Metro system.

The world's first public railway line to use steam locomotives, the Stockton & Darlington Railway initially connected collieries near Shildon with Stockton-on-Tees and Darlington – its first steam-hauled passenger train on 27 September 1825 being pulled by George Stephenson's *Locomotion No.1*. For its many years in preservation in Darlington Station, *Locomotion No.1* carried the name *Locomotion 1825* to mark its place in railway history.

But while passengers were certainly an important part of the company's business plan, the railway's main function was initially the transportation of coal.

The Stockton & Darlington was not the first passenger railway, but it was the first to use steam locomotives. Eighteen years earlier in 1807, the world's first passenger train service had opened between Swansea and Oystermouth in South Wales (*qv*), with the trains hauled by horses.

The first steam train on the S&DR had just one passenger coach – called *Experiment* – carrying just 18 passengers, with the remainder of the train comprising 21 brand new coal wagons, fitted with seats specially for the occasion.

below left: An early postcard of Shildon Station declaring it to be the 'Oldest Railway Station', having been opened in 1825 as part of the Stockton & Darlington Railway. Today the station – now completely un-manned – primarily serves the Shildon site of the National Railway Museum.

bottom: Looking more like a rural farmhouse than a railway station, Allendale Station near Hexham in Northumberland can trace it origins back to 1868 when it was opened as Catton Road, the terminus of a branch-line, by the Hexham & Allendale Railway. Built primarily to transport lead from local mines to the main line at Hexham, passenger services started around 1876, by which time the line was operated by the North Eastern Railway. Catton Road was renamed Allendale Station in 1898. The line was abandoned in 1950, but passenger services had been withdrawn twenty years ealier. The platform and station buildings still stand adjacent to Allendale Caravan Park, the waiting rooms now converted into a self-catering holiday apartment.

Shildon, Oldest Railway Station

Railway Station, Allendale

Midland Station, Masboro

above: Postcards of Rotherham's four-platform Midland Railway Station survive with three different spellings of the name – 'Masboro', 'Masbrough', and 'Masborough'. From 1896 the station was known as 'Rotherham Masborough' and was the *de facto* main station for the town until closure in 1987 when services were transferred to Rotherham Central.

right: Known as Class C1 Large Boiler Atlantics, these Ivatt-designed locomotives were introduced on to the Great Northern Railway in 1902. 94 were built between 1902 and 1910.

Railway overcrowding is clearly nothing new – the train was intended to carry 300 passengers but, according to reports, it set off on that first journey with somewhere between 450 and 600 people on board.

For the next eight years, while the coal trains were locomotive-hauled, most passenger trains were horse-drawn just as they were in Wales. It was not until 1833 that regular steam-hauled passenger trains took over.

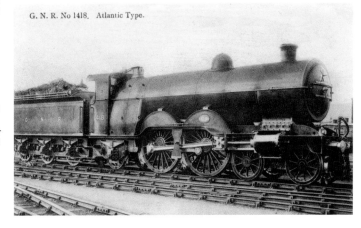

G. N. R. No 1418. Atlantic Type.

INTERIOR OF MIDLAND STATION, BRADFORD

By the time the Stockton & Darlington Railway company was absorbed into the North Eastern Railway in 1863, its network extended for around 200 route miles, and it had amassed a very large fleet of locomotives and rolling stock.

While on the streets, the pace of life in those days was still dictated by the trotting speed of a horse and the walking speed of a man, on the railways the maturing network and faster trains democratised travel and made it ever more accessible to the masses.

Successive mergers amongst the many Victorian companies which had pioneered railway travel in the region top: Despite being captioned 'Railway Station, Crook', this postcard from c.1910 is more a study of the infrastructure which served Joseph Pease's nearby Roddymoor Colliery, Bank Foot Coke Works, Chemical Plant, and fire clay works in County Durham. The station had just the single platform seen here, and had originally been opened by the Stockton & Darlington Railway in 1844. Both passenger and freight traffic reduced dramatically in the 1930s, around the same time that Roddymoor Colliery closed, but the station remained open until the Beeching cuts in the 1960s.

right: Thirsk Station was opened by the Great North of England Railway in 1841 and was originally known as Newcastle Junction, but by 1848 had been renamed Thirsk Junction. The station, now known simply as Thirsk, remains open today.

had, by the end of the nineteenth century, heralded the emergence of expanded networks controlled by a few big operators. That had seen the majority of services operated by the Lancashire & Yorkshire Railway, the Great Northern, the North Eastern, the Midland, the Great Central and the London & North Western, with other smaller companies having negotiated access rights. Managing a network with so many different operators was a challenging undertaking.

For postcard collectors, however, cards which show everyday routines and traffic movements are the ones which really bring the Edwardian railways to life – especially those which illustrate unexpected aspects of the infrastructure of the network.

That even a relatively short line such as that between Hull and Withernsea should have its own turntable was considered unusual enough for it to be the subject of a 1906 postcard, *below*. The manually-operated small turntable was constructed some time well after the NER took ownership of the line in 1862, and after it had been extended from Victoria Dock Station through to Hull Paragon Station in 1864. On many branch lines, a returning train would usually have run tender first.

Perhaps not surprisingly, accidents were not uncommon, but while they certainly gave photographers the chance to take and publish some dramatic images as postcards, relatively few of them resulted in fatalities. Most were put down to human error in the enquiries which inevitably followed, the others ascribed to equipment failure.

Within the time frame embraced by this book, seven major accidents took place – a relatively small number given the many thousands of train movements which were undertaken daily. The worst of them was described as driver error in thick fog, when a danger signal was passed.

below: The single-platform Withernsea Station was the terminus of a 17.5 mile line from Hull to the east coast resort, and was opened in 1854 by the short-lived Hull & Holderness Railway. By 1862 the H&HR had been absorbed by the North Eastern Railway. The line initially terminated at the York & North Midland Railway's Victoria Dock Station in Hull, but was later extended into Hull Paragon. The locomotive on the turntable in this postcard is a Wilson Worsdell-designed NER M1 Class 4-4-0 locomotive, built at Gateshead and dating from the mid-1890s.

right: The elegant station buildings at Birstwith, on the 14 mile single-track branch-line between Harrogate and Pateley Bridge, were built by the North Eastern Railway and opened to traffic in 1862. The station was closed to passenger trains in 1951 and goods traffic in 1964.

middle: Netherton Station was opened by the Lancashire & Yorkshire Railway at the end of the Netherton Tunnel on its Meltham branch line. Passenger services operated along the single-track line from 1869. Never commercially viable, the line was closed to passengers in 1949 and just a few traces of the station remain.

bottom: When Crossgates Station was opened by the Leeds & Selby Railway in 1834, Crossgates was a small village a few miles from Leeds. The station closed after six years, only to be re-opened by the L&SR in 1850, by which time traffic was increasing. It was rebuilt by the North Eastern Railway in 1902 two years before this postcard was published. It is now known as Cross Gates.

left: South Shields Station was opened in 1879 by the North Eastern Railway with services to Newcastle. It was closed in 1981 when a new Metro station was built. This postcard was published c.1906.

below: Cliff House Junction and Ironworks, West Hartlepool, on the North Eastern Railway. The West Hartlepool Steel & Iron Company opened the ironworks in 1860. By the time this postcard was published in 1908, the company was part of the South Durham Steel & Iron Company. The works were closed by British Steel in 1977.

That accident happened on 19 January 1905 with *The Spectator,* just two days later, reporting that 'A terrible accident occurred on the Midland Railway near Cudworth Junction, between Leeds and Sheffield, early on Thursday morning. The Scotch up express, drawn by two engines, and travelling at fifty miles an hour, ran into a mail train from Leeds to Sheffield, travelling slowly in the same direction and on the same rails. Both trains were completely wrecked and caught

right: A locally
produced postcard
of the aftermath of
the Waleswood train
crash south of
Rotherham on
17 January 1912
involving a Great
Central Railway
train, the cause of
which was ascribed
to suspension failure
and 'poor design'.

middle & bottom:
The accident at
Woodhouse near
Sheffield on 29
February 1908
resulted in two
deaths and five
serious injuries. In
dense fog, a train
taking 300 emigrants
from Liverpool to
Grimsby, drawn by
Pollitt-designed
Class 11 locomotives
No.711 and 852, ran
into the rear of a
goods train in a
dense fog. Local
photographers
Warner Gothard
of Barnsley were
early on the scene,
producing one of
their hallmark
photo-composite
cards which included
portraits of the dead
fireman from No.711
and the goods train
guard, as well as
711's injured driver.

RAILWAY COLLISION AT HUDDERSFIELD. GOOD-FRIDAY, APRIL 1905. (x2.)   COPYRIGHT.

left: The accident at Huddersfield on Good Friday, 21 April 1905, occurred between a London & North Western passenger train and Lancashire & Yorkshire train shunting empty carriages. Two people were killed and thirteen injured. The train being shunted had passed a danger signal.

fire, and the down Scotch express was only just pulled up in time before running into the wreckage. Few passengers were travelling in the wrecked trains, but six persons were killed on the spot, including two boys who were returning to Bradfield College, another died during the day, and fifteen were injured, seven seriously.'

On 21 April that same year, an L&NWR train also passed a danger signal in fog – near Huddersfield – and exactly the same combination of fog and driver error was given as the cause of a crash on the North Eastern Railway, at Ulleskelf south of Tadcaster, on 24 November 1906. There is much to be said for today's electronic safety systems.

bottom: A Great Central Railway 0-6-0 tender locomotive running tender first and pulling 44 full coal wagons, 12 empties and a brake van, collided with a shunting goods train at Wombwell near Barnsley on 13 December 1911. When the runaway train crashed, the wagons disintegrated showering coal everywhere and burying the forty-nine-year old driver and his twenty-three-year old fireman. Both died. The official report on the accident summarised the cause as inadequate brakes. Each alternate loaded wagon should have had its brakes applied before approaching the gradient, but only a few had. Some estimated that the train's speed approached 60mph instead of the normal 4mph.

IRVING   G.C RAILWAY SMASH WOMBWELL DEC 15 1911

THE NORTH-WEST

MANCHESTER'S LIVERPOOL ROAD STATION – the first purpose-built inter-city passenger railway terminus in the world – is today one of the city's most popular tourist destinations, its vast warehouses – some of which date from the reign of King William IV – long-since restored to their original magnificence and adapted for use as Manchester's Museum of Science and Industry. It was built in 1830 by the Liverpool & Manchester Railway, and only used for a few years before the construction of Victoria Station by the Manchester & Leeds Railway. By 1844 Liverpool Road's days as a terminus were over and the L&MR had transferred its services into Victoria.

By the late 1840s, Victoria Station had 16 platforms, and most of the trains operating out of it were run by the Lancashire & Yorkshire Railway. A large tile mural showing the company's network still graces the entrance to the station. The station, now reduced to just six platforms, was restored in 2009 and given a new roof over the main concourse replacing the original damaged by the 1996 bomb.

opposite: From a postcard of the Excursion Platforms at Euston Road Station, Morecambe, c.1904, as visitors from the mill towns of Lancashire arrived to start their holidays.

below: A lively scene at Crewe Station, already one of the country's busiest junctions. From a postcard c.1905.

overleaf: The erecting shop at the Lancashire & Yorkshire Railway's locomotive works at Horwich. From a series of L&YR 'Official' postcards.

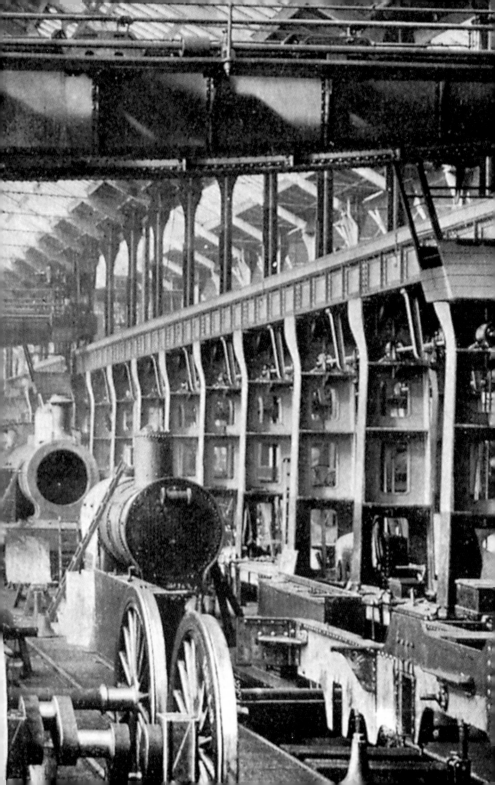

right: A 13 inch gauge
engine hauling a
locomotive boiler at
Horwich Works —
an L&YR 'Official'
postcard from 1905.

below: A postcard
print, believed to
show a railwayman
from the Wigan area,
photographed in his
back yard c.1910.

The L&YR had been created by
the merger of nineteen smaller
railway companies, all set up since
1830, the investors in each having
firmly believed – initially at least –
that railways were their ticket to
untold riches. Few of them ever saw
any return on their investment. The
L&YR would absorb a further fifteen
companies – each of which had
required the passing of a separate
Act of Parliament to approve its
establishment.

right: A Lancashire
& Yorkshire Railway
Hughes-designed
steam railmotor, built
at the Horwich Works
in 1906.

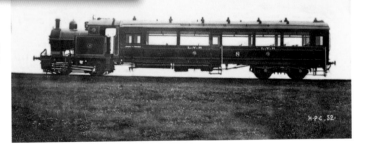

Cark in Cartmel. Railway Station.

Fleetwood Railway Station.

left: Cark in Cartmel Station, seen here in 1904, has had three different names since opened by the Ulverston & Lancaster Railway in 1857. It was originally known as Cark-in-Cartmell, before the last 'l' was dropped. The 19.5 mile line was taken over by the Furness Railway in 1862. Since 1906, it has been known as Cark and Cartmel.

below left: The first railway station in Fleetwood was opened in Dock Street by the Preston & Wyre Joint Railway in 1840 as the terminus of their line from Preston. This was before a cross-border line was completed to Scotland, so tourists heading north travelled by train to Fleetwood and then by steamer to Ardrossan on the Ayrshire coast. The station illustrated here opened in Queen's Terrace in 1883, carrying passengers to and from the Irish steamers, but they arrived at an outside platform rather than under the station's fine glass canopy. It was closed in 1966 by Beeching, services being re-routed to Wyre Dock Station — renamed Fleetwood — until it closed in 1970.

In 1884, the directors of the L&YR made a momentous decision – to design and build their own locomotives in-house – and purchased a large site at Horwich near Bolton. The vast loco works they built there became one of the area's major employers and, under the guidance of Chief Engineer John Aspinall, their first locomotive, a 2-4-2 tank engine given the railway number 1008, rolled out of the works in 1889. It survives in the National Railway Museum in York.

Like Beyer Peacock's Gorton works – where a number of the L&YR's locomotives had been built, Horwich had its own team of photographers on hand to photograph each new right: Barney the Goose with friends on the quayside at Whitehaven in October 1901, issued as a postcard c.1904. The Hudswell-Clarke locomotive behind the group, named *Edward VII*, was one of four built by the Hunslet company for the narrow-gauge Derry & Lough Swilly Railway Company. The locomotive was about to be shipped to Ireland for use on the line between Carndonough and Burtonport.

below: Manning Wardle's 1876-built 3ft gauge 0-6-0 tank engine *Nabb Gill*, Works No.629, at Boot Station on the Ravenglass & Eskdale Railway in Cumbria, c.1905.

design as it was out-shopped and, when picture postcards came along the whole locomotive-building process was celebrated in a series of popular cards.

At the same time, the London & North Western Railway – which would later absorb the L&YR – was also producing 'Official' postcards of many aspects of its operations.

Huge numbers of locomotives were exported across the world during the Edwardian era from both Liverpool and

SILLOTH STATION AND DOCKS.

left: Silloth Docks and Station in Cumbria were opened in 1856 on the Carlisle & Silloth Bay Railway's line from Carlisle. The C&SBR became part of the North British Railway in 1880.

below: A glimpse of the London & North Western Railway's Lime Street Station in Liverpool, seen behind a crowd watching a Punch and Judy Show c.1910. The station originally opened as the terminus of the Liverpool & Manchester Railway in 1836, but the present building with its huge arched canopy roof, was completed by the London & North Western Railway in 1849.

Manchester docks – built not just by Beyer Peacock, but also by the huge Vulcan Foundry in Newton-le-Willows.

The L&NWR's Crewe Works, originally opened in 1840 by the Grand Junction Railway, turned out some of the finest locomotives in Britain. At its peak it employed over 20,000 people, but today just a small repair faclity survives.

The North-West's place in railway history is right up there. After all, the Liverpool & Manchester Railway had opened as long ago as 1830, and amongst its locomotives were George Stephenson's *Rocket* – the most famous of all the early locomotives, a working replica of which took part in the re-enactment of the famous Rainhill Trials in 1981.

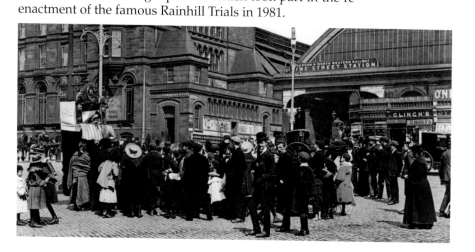

right: Manchester's London Road Station was opened as Store Street in 1842, renamed London Road in 1847, its name changed again to Manchester Piccadilly when completely rebuilt in 1960. At the time this postcard was published in 1902, it was used by the London & North Western Railway and the Great Central Railway, which had taken over the Manchester, Sheffield & Lincolnshire Railway in 1897.

below: Opened in 1880 by the Cheshire Lines Railway, Manchester Central was closed in 1969 and is now an exhibition venue.

Also seen at Rainhill in 1980 was an original L&MR survivor – *Lion* – built in 1837 and now preserved in the Museum of Liverpool.

In September 1830, on the opening day of the Liverpool & Manchester Railway, William Huskisson became the first person in the world to be killed by a passenger train.

London Road Station Manchester

Central Station, Manchester.

98

above: The Electric Parcels Carrier in Manchester's Victoria Station, from a Lancashire & Yorkshire Railway official series postcard published c.1904. The carrier, designed by the railway's Chief Mechanical Engineer John Aspinall in the 1890s, linked the parcels depot directly with the station's main platforms. The driver was often suspended more than 20 feet up in the air. Aspinall was the L&YR's CME from 1886 until 1899.

Huskisson was travelling as a passenger with the Duke of Wellington, but disembarked at Parkside Station near Newton-le-Willows, to talk to acquaintances. He walked across the line in front of an on-coming train intending to greet a friend and was killed when he fell under the wheels of *Rocket*. Before him, elsewhere, two men had, a little earlier, been separately killed by goods trains.

By the time the Vulcan Foundry closed in 1962, it had built several thousand locomotives in its 130-year history. The site has now largely been redeveloped for housing.

Beyer Peacock & Company built 8000 locomotives and shipped the majority of them overseas during 112 years of manufacture before closing the Gorton plant in 1966.

The Horwich Works had a life of less than eighty years, ceasing locomotive building in 1965, and the majority of that site has also now been redeveloped.

But during its operational life, some of steam railway's most innovative designers had learned their engineering skills within its walls – including Sir Nigel Gresley, who would later design both the *Flying Scotsman* and the streamlined A4 Pacifics for the LNER in the course of his eminent career.

right: With the opening of a rail tunnel under the Mersey in 1886, Liverpool became the first city outside of London to have an underground railway. The system was electrified in 1903, and this postcard was produced around the time of its re-opening.

middle: Hamilton Square, one of the deep underground stations on the Mersey Railway, was accessed by lifts.

bottom:
The Sheffield, Ashton-under-Lyne & Manchester Railway opened Broadbottom station in 1842, but just three years later changed the name to Mottram. In 1847 the line was taken over by the Manchester, Sheffield & Lincolnshire Railway who eventually renamed the station once again, becoming 'Mottram and Broadbottom' in 1884. In 1897, the MS&LR became the Great Central Railway. In the Edwardian era, at least three different 'Blackfriars Series' postcard views were on sale. The station still operates today, albeit minus the footbridge in this 1906 view, and is once again known as Broadbottom.

An Electric Train on the Mersey Railway.

Birkenhead.

The Wrench Series, No. 7571

Hamilton Square Station.

MOTTRAM & BROADBOTTOM

Marple Station — Midland Railway

left: Marple Station was opened in 1865 by the Manchester, Sheffield & Lincolnshire Railway, serving their line between Hyde in Cheshire and New Mills in Derbyshire. The station was also served by Midland Railway trains. By the time this postcard was published, the MS&LR had 'rebranded' itself as the Great Central Railway, a name change made in 1897.

The areas around Manchester and Liverpool were criss-crossed with hundreds of lines by the beginning of the twentieth century, transporting the vast output of goods from the region's mines, mills and factories, and also playing key roles in the movement of people – both to and from work, and on the annual staggered Wakes Week holidays.

On holiday Saturdays, the platforms of stations in Wigan, Oldham, Rochdale, Bolton, Preston and elsewhere would be thronging with people eager to escape the drudgery of the mills and factories for a week, while coastal resorts such as Blackpool and Morecambe even built separate 'excursion platforms' to cater for the annual influx of holidaymakers.

below: Port Carlisle Station in Cumbria was actually part of Scotland's North British Railway. Opened in 1854 by the Port Carlisle Dock & Railway Company, the 11-mile line was built to carry goods to Port Carlisle, but demand for a passenger service resulted in horse-drawn 'Dandy Cars' being introduced. From 1862 the NBR operated the service and fully absorbed the company in 1880. Four Dandy Cars were used until steam was introduced in April 1914. One of the restored coaches – used for years as the clubhouse for a bowls club – is now preserved in the National Railway Museum, York.

Port Carlisle Station

right: A pair of Class 890 locomotives double-head the Midland Railway's 'Scotch Express' as it prepares to leave Carlisle and climb Beatock Summit.

middle & bottom: Two postcards of Northwich Station in Cheshire 1906-1910, opened by the Cheshire Midland Railway in 1863. The company ran into financial difficulties early on and sought support from both the Manchester Sheffield & Lincolnshire Railway, and the Great Northern. By 1865 all three had formed the Cheshire Lines Committee to operate routes around Manchester and Cheshire and as far north as Wigan.

Scotch Express leaving Carlisle Station

Northwich Station.

Out of season, those parts of the stations would be completely closed off, but throughout the summer, as each town took its annual Wakes Week holiday in turn, special trains would sometimes have to queue outside the resorts' stations to get platform access, so great were the numbers of visitors – all of them arriving and leaving on Saturdays.

Today, Blackpool North Station stands on the site of the former Talbot Road excursion platforms, while Blackpool Central has gone, and Morecambe's two Edwardian stations have both been replaced by one – those changes reflecting the fact that most of today's holidaymakers make their way to the coast not by train, but along the M6 and the M55.

below left: Oldham once boasted no fewer than six railway stations — a remarkable number for a town of its size. Central Station was one of the casualties of the rationalisation of the 1960s, and hardly a trace of it remains today. It was opened in 1847 by the newly renamed Lancashire & Yorkshire Railway, having been planned by the Manchester & Leeds Railway as one of the stations on a branchline from their main route. This card dates from around 1906. The station closed to passenger traffic in 1966.

bottom: Heysham Harbour Station offered connections with steamers to Belfast, Scotland and the Isle of Man. Opened by the Midland Railway in 1904, with services using two steam railmotors built at Derby especially for the route, it was still very new when this postcard was produced. By 1908, the line had been electrified, so this card predates the installation of the overhead catenary.

Central Station, Oldham.

top: Opened by the Manchester & Birmingham Railway as Alderley Station in 1843 — and later renamed Alderley and Chorley in 1853, the station on the main line between Manchester and Crewe did not assume its current name until the line was taken over by the London & North Western Railway in 1876.

middle: Altrincham Station — the town's second railway station — was opened in April 1881 by the Manchester, South Junction & Altrincham Railway and originally known as 'Altrincham & Bowdon'. The company's line from the Cheshire town to Manchester's London Road Station had been opened in 1849.

bottom: *Coronation*, a 4-4-0 superheated express engine, was built at Crewe in 1910 by the L&NWR as the first of their George the Fifth Class and named in honour of the new King's coronation. It was designed by the company's CME, Charles Bowen-Cooke. None of the class survived into preservation, but a new-build, to be known as No.2013 *Prince George*, is currently under construction.

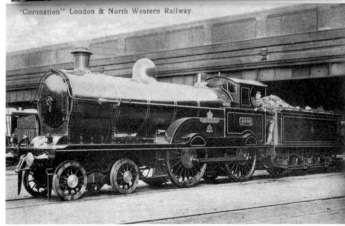

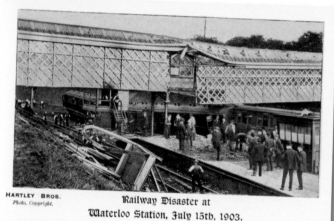

HARTLEY BROS.
Photo. Copyright.

Railway Disaster at
Waterloo Station, July 15th, 1903.

above: Carnforth Station — seen here c.1906 — had been planned by the Lancashire & Carlisle Railway, but the L&CR had been taken over by the London & North Western before it opened in 1846. Almost a century after it first opened, the station was used as the setting for the 1945 film *Brief Encounter*.

left: On 15 July 1903, a Lancashire & Yorkshire Railway train, approaching Liverpool's Waterloo Station too fast, was derailed. It collided with the station footbridge at speed, killing seven people and injuring 116.

Around the Great Manchester area, several former railway lines have been redeveloped for use as part of the city's Metrolink tram system. With in excess of 37,000,000 passenger journeys a year over nearly 100km of track, it is now the largest light railway system in Britain – and still growing. A completely new route to Trafford Park is currently under construction.

WALES

THE OYSTERMOUTH RAILWAY – a 6-mile line running between Swansea and Oystermouth – was Britain's, and the world's, first passenger-carrying railway. It carried its first fare-paying passengers in late March 1807, more than eighteen years before anyone bought a ticket to travel on Robert Stephenson's much more widely celebrated Stockton & Darlington Railway in the North-east of England.

Originally laid to a 4ft gauge, passengers were carried in modified stagecoaches on rails pulled by horses, but after twenty years, the service was withdrawn, the line then being used exclusively for goods traffic.

That remained the case for a further twenty years before the railway – by this time using steam locomotives and running on standard-gauge track – once again carried passengers. Re-named the Swansea & Mumbles Railway in 1893 – it had long been simply known locally as the 'Mumbles Train' – the line survived until closure in 1960.

The mad dash to build railways in more remote corners of Victorian Wales, whether or not there was any real commercial rationale for so doing, is epitomised by memories of long-abandoned lines in many places where difficult terrain, and small, scattered and remote populations, made the likelihood of turning a profit as remote as some of the stations themselves.

opposite top: The Swansea & Mumbles Railway's locomotive No.4 at the head of a five-car train, c.1904. The line's locomotives were built by Falcon Engine Works, Manning Wardle, Hunslet, Black Hawthorn, and Avonside, and were either 0-4-0T or 0-6-0T tank engines. Two of them were named *Crumlyn* and *Swansea*.

opposite bottom: Always known as 'the Mumbles train' the line was officially a 'light railway' or 'tramway'. In this postcard c.1907, the double-decked cars certainly look more like trams than railway coaches.

below: The postcard, captioned "Off to the Mumbles" was based on a photograph taken in 1899. It was published – in sepia or tinted as here – probably in 1902. At the head of the train is locomotive No.5, built in the late 1870s. The line was electrified in 1929, running tramcars with overhead catenary, and was eventually closed completely in 1960.

below right: The novel design of the Britannia Bridge across the Menai Strait between North Wales and Anglesey, made it a popular subject for postcards. Robert Stephenson's innovative tubular bridge was completed in 1849 and opened the following year. A fire in 1970 led to the total destruction of the bridge, which was subsequently rebuilt to a very different design.

below: Llandovery Station, opened in 1858 by the Vale of Towy Railway was, when this postcard was published c.1904, jointly operated by the L&NWR and the GWR.

During the nineteenth century, no fewer than 73 railway companies – each requiring the passing of a separate Act of Parliament – had been established, and by 1900 the majority of those in South Wales had already been absorbed, through successive mergers, into the Great Western.

Several of those lines remained independent for just a few years, the shortest-lived probably being the Cardiff & Ogmore Railway – a mineral line authorised in 1873 – which was absorbed into the Llynfi & Ogmore Railway, already operated by the GWR, less than three years later.

By the dawn of the picture postcard era, railways in Wales were dominated by the Great Western. Indeed several of the

Britannia Tubular Bridge, North Wales
Total cost, £600,000. Length of Tubes to Central Tower, 460 feet each.
Length of Tubes to the Abutment, 230 feet each.

Llandovery Station.

The Taff Railway Station, Mountain Ash

left: Mountain Ash Station was opened by the Taff Vale Railway on their Aberdare branchline in 1888, but of the station illustrated in this postcard c.1906, little trace remains. It was closed to passengers in 1964 only to be re-opened in 1988, with a new station built in 2002.

below: Bridgend Station was opened in 1850 on the Great Western Railway's Paddington to Swansea main line. Passenger services on the branchlines which terminated at the station were withdrawn in the 1960s and '70s but have been successfully reinstated in recent years.

lines which had still retained their individual identities were not really independent, being managed and operated by the GWR.

There was, of course, also a significant presence for the London & North Western Railway – largely in North Wales – and the Midland Railway which ran into Swansea. In North Wales, by 1912, every standard-gauge line was controlled either by the GWR or the London & North Western Railway.

Railway Station, Bridgend

right: Llanwrtyd Station in Powys was opened by the London & North Western Railway in 1867 as part of their drive into mid Wales, and was on their route linking Shrewsbury with Swansea. The station remains in use today, and has one of five passing loops on an otherwise single track line.

bottom: The London & North Western Railway's double-headed Irish Mail train from Holyhead to London Euston passing a pick-up at Colwyn Bay around 1905. The service was first introduced in 1848.

Station, Llanwrtyd Wells.

The L&NWR's reach stretched into South Wales as well, with the opening of a branch line from the Merthyr, Tredegar & Abergavenny Railway – which the L&NWR already controlled – to Ebbw Vale in 1867.

There was, however, already a station in Ebbw Vale, operated by the Monmouthshire Railway & Canal Company, offering direct services to Newport since the 1850s.

The L&NWR station – the terminus of their branch line from Beaufort was also named Ebbw Vale, creating a confusion which lasted until nationalisation when it was renamed Ebbw Vale (High Level) and the older station Ebbw Vale (Low Level). So, despite once timetabling more than

COLWYN BAY. IRISH MAIL TAKING IN BAGS

L. and N.W. Railway Station and Wesleyan Chapel, Ebbw Vale

Railway Station, Ebbw Vale.

M.J.R.B. 6292.

above: The London & North Western Railway's Ebbw Vale Station was the terminus of their branch line from Beaufort. It was closed to passengers in 1951 and subsequently a multi-storey car park was built on the site. That has now been replaced by a shopping mall.

left: Ebbw Vale's other station was opened by the Monmouthshire Railway & Canal Company in 1852. By 1875 all trains were being operated by the Great Western, which absorbed the MR&C in 1880. Passenger services were withdrawn in 1962 with complete closure in 1969.

thirty trains a day, it was never as popular with passengers, although heavily used for freight.

The L&NWR station was closed to passengers in 1951, and to goods eight years later, the site of the station now occupied by a shopping centre. The site of the low level station – closed to passengers in 1962 – now lies beneath a road which uses part of the trackbed.

right: Llanrhaiadr Station was opened in 1862 by the Denbigh, Ruthin & Corwen Railway, which by 1879 had become a constituent company of the London & North Western Railway. Passenger trains were withdrawn in 1953 and freight nine years later.

bottom: The London & North Western Railway's Station Hotel at Holyhead opened in 1880. Adjacent to the station, it had 75 rooms and its own golf course. The total cost of building both the hotel and the station was just £65,000. The hotel closed in 1951 and was demolished in 1979, replaced by the office block known as Stena House.

Railway Station, Llanrhaiadr, near Denbigh

Station Hotel, Holyhead

Passenger services to the town were restored in 2008, using some of the original Monmouthshire Railway & Canal Company's trackbed, but with newly-built stations.

The volume of traffic in the first few years has far exceeded expectations, prompting the Welsh Government to initiate plans to reverse other closures, but the railway map of Wales can never be restored to anything like what it was before wholesale closures were started after the end of the Second World War.

Many stations had been closed long before Dr Beeching's report was published in 1963. Rhayader Station in Cwmdauddwr, Powys, was just one of the many such casualties. Built by the Mid Wales Railway and opened in 1864, it survived until just two years short of its centenary.

In total, the Welsh railway network today extends for around 800 route miles, a far cry from its Edwardian heyday when the total passenger route mileage was probably close to double that. Despite widespread belief that most of the closures were down to Beeching, he was responsible for the ending of passenger services along about 250 route miles –

right: The Mid-Wales Railway opened Rhayader Station in 1864 but the line experienced financial difficulties from the outset. It was eventually absorbed into the Cambrian Railways group in 1904 with whom it had had a working agreement since 1888.

bottom: The London & North Western Railway built six 43-ton, 48-seat, 'Steam Rail Motor Coaches' between 1905 and 1907 for use on lines in Oxfordshire and North Wales. This view on the single track Prestatyn to Dyserth branchline was published as a postcard c.1908.

RAILWAY STATION, RHAYADER.

Prestatyn to Dyserth by motor.

top: When Irish Sea ferry services started from Fishguard in 1906, the station's importance grew considerably. Three years later Transatlantic Liners started to visit the port, the first Cunarder to do so being the RMS *Mauretania* in August that year. The Great Western laid on a special service to transport passengers to and from the port the first 'Mauretania Express' being hauled by locomotives 3402 *Halifax* and 4108 *Gardenia*.

middle: Porth Station, as seen in this postcard c.1905, was the second station to serve the Rhondda Valley town, the original 1861 station being closed and replaced after just fifteen years. The line between Barry and Porth was opened and operated by the Taff Valley Railway.

bottom: Valley Station on Anglesey — the penultimate stop on the London & North Western Railway's North Wales Coast line to Holyhead — was opened in 1849, and remains in use today.

left: A once-typical scene as railways criss-crossed the Welsh Valleys. The bridge is the viaduct at Aberbargoed in the Rhymney Valley in the heart of mining country.

bottom: Rhyl Station was opened in 1848 on the Chester & Holyhead Railway's main line from Chester to Bangor along the North Wales coast. A separate line ran from Llanfair PG to Holyhead, the two being linked in 1850, with the opening of Stephenson's Britannia Bridge. The C&HR was taken over by the London & North Western Railway in 1858.

but while they may not have been considered viable from a commercial point of view, they were hugely important miles, leaving large parts of the country – especially West Wales – either with a fragmented service, or completely cut off from the national rail network.

Most significant of the cuts was probably the axing of the Carmarthen to Aberystwyth line, originally operated by the GWR and its subsidiaries. In 2017, feasibility studies funded by the Welsh Government have been instigated to determine the potential for reopening the route.

Some measure of the scale of freight traffic can be gleaned from the number of locomotives and rolling stock operated

Railway Station, Rhyl

The Station, Llangollen

523 71

above: Llangollen
Station opened to
passenger traffic in
1865, replacing an
earlier station on the
outskirts of the
town. Another victim
of Beeching's
'rationalisation' of
Welsh railways, the
station closed in
1965. Since 1891 it
has been reborn as
the terminus of the
heritage Llangollen
Railway which now
operates steam
services along a 9½
mile section of the
former Barmouth
line.

by even relatively small companies. By 1910 the Rhymney Railway, which operated routes in South Wales, north from Cardiff and up into the Welsh coalfields, is estimated to have owned and operated around 120 locomotives – a remarkable number for a relatively compact network.

To most people today, however, the most celebrated railways in Wales are the many preserved narrow-gauge lines, built to an assortment of gauges around 2 feet (600-610mm) which were originally laid to access slate quarries and other mineral sites.

Horse drawn mineral railways in North Wales can be traced back to 1836, but the first steam-hauled service, Festiniog & Blaenau Railway, opened in 1868, followed by the London & North Western Railway's standard gauge line to the slate quarries in 1873 – and a year later the GWR-backed Bala & Festiniog Railway also opened.

By 1883 the B&FR had abandoned narrow gauge and it too had been relaid by the GWR to standard gauge.

Prince and *Palmerston*, two of the Festiniog Railway's Victorian 0-4-0STT locomotives, built by George England & Co of New Cross in 1864, are still in use on the line today.

Effect of Slip on the Officials' Houses, New Tredegar.

left: One of a series of cards published c.1910, recording the impact of a landslip adjacent to a mineral line at New Tredegar.

bottom: Bargoed Station, Glamorgan, was opened in 1858 by the Rhymney Railway, which remained independent until it merged with the GWR in 1922. The station was once a busy junction and services were shared with the London & North Western. It originally had three platforms but today just two survive. This card was posted in 1907, by which time the station was actually known as Bargoed and Aber Bargoed.

These railways carried millions of tons of minerals to Welsh ports, and when usurped by the lorry, turned their secondary income stream – passengers – into their first.

Passengers – both workers and tourists – had been carried since the late Victorian years, and when the picture postcard came along, Wales's little railways were amongst the first to see the tourist potential of the tinted card.

The Station, Bargoed.

right: The Glyn Valley Railway, also known as the Glyn Valley Tramway, was an 8-mile narrow-gauge line linking Chirk and Glyn Ceiriog in North Wales. It opened in 1880 and was built primarily as a mineral line to move materials from the quarries at Glyn Ceriog to the Shropshire Union Canal at Chirk. Passenger trains operated along just over 6 miles of the route from 1888. The locomotive at the head of this train, *Sir Theodore*, was an 0-4-2T built by Beyer Peacock at Gorton, Manchester, in 1888 and worked the line until 1905.

middle & below: The narrow gauge Vale of Rheidol Light Railway opened in 1902 running services along the 12 mile route between Aberystwyth and Devil's Bridge, initially with two locomotives. No.1 *Edward VII*, was scrapped in 1932. No.2, named *Prince of Wales* and seen *above middle* in a c.1903 postcard, was withdrawn in 1923 and replaced by a near identical locomotive built by the GWR's Swindon Works. The GWR had taken the line over that year.

Glyn Valley Train   Photo by Burns

On the Way to Devil's Bridge

ABERYSTWYTH STATION, RHEIDOL RAILWAY.

top: Snowdon Railway locomotives were all built with their boilers angled forwards to counter the effects of the steep gradient. *Enid*, one of the original 1895 locomotives, built by the Swiss Locomotive and Machine Works of Winterthur, is still in regular service today.

middle: An unidentified locomotive approaching the summit. The train was always pushed up the gradient.

bottom: Locomotive No.4, *Snowdon*, was built in 1896, also by the Swiss Locomotive and Machine Works. It is currently not in service, awaiting a major overhaul.

CALEDONIAN RAILWAY

TO THE STEAMERS

BOOKING OFFICE

Glasgow Train at Gourock Pier

SCOTLAND

IN 1955, MY FAMILY MOVED FROM STIRLING to the little Perthshire village of Braco. We didn't have a car, but there was an infrequent bus service in and out of the village and, just over a mile's walk away in the hamlet of Greenloaning, there was a railway station on the Stirling to Perth main line. The next year, like so many other small halts across the country, the station closed and was later demolished, bringing to an end a railway history going back over a century.

Also known as 'Greenloaning for Braco', the station had been opened by the Scottish Central Railway on 22 May 1848, at a time when the commercial potential of rural stations like this was hugely over-estimated.

Although it only closed to passengers on 11 June 1956, it had probably never been viable throughout its existence and the majority of trains had no longer stopped there for years anyway.

Around 1905 – by then operated by the Caledonian Railway – Greenloaning, like most stations in Britain, got its own series of picture postcards to sell to waiting passengers.

opposite: Detail from a postcard showing the entrance from the steamer pier to the Caledonian Railway's new Wemyss Bay Station, opened in 1903. *(for full card see p20)*

inset: A Caledonian Railways train bound for Glasgow in 1906, hauled by Drummond Class 80 No.116, built at St Rollox Works in 1888. The railway's steamers operated several routes from Gourock.

below: Wemyss Bay Station and steamer pier, a composite postcard from 1910.

GREENLOANING STATION, BRACO

above: Greenloaning Station as it looked from the main road bridge c.1906.

At least four different Edwardian cards have been identified.

What is remarkable is that so many of the cards on sale at rural stations were printed in colour, using a process which required much larger sales to show a profit than cheaper monochrome or sepia views. The Greenloaning postcards were produced by Valentine of Dundee, the biggest postcard publisher in Scotland, and one of the biggest in Britain.

Valentines were canny operators, so must have believed that there was going to be a sufficient number of people willing to buy and write a postcard while seated on the platform benches – the Edwardian equivalent of the irritating and pointless 'I'm just waiting for the train' text message of today. Except that in the postcard photograph, there are no passengers waiting on the platform, just two railway employees – and no train!

The publishers were willing to go to the expense of producing the card, but the photographer saw no necessity in waiting for a train to arrive.

Needless to say, the postcard was not a commercial success, and it was still on sale in Braco Post Office fifty years later, as were some multi-view tinted cards of the village from the same era.

left: A Dundee-bound train about to depart from Wormit Station to cross over the 'new' Tay Bridge c.1904. The bases of the piers of the ill-fated first bridge can still be seen today.

below: The paddle steamer *Princess May* at Balloch Pier at the southern tip of Loch Lomond. The vessel was operated by The Loch Lomond Steamboat Company, a subsidiary of the North British Railway Company. Standing alongside at Balloch Pier Station is a Caledonian Railway train from Glasgow. The station had been opened in 1850 by the Caledonian & Dunbartonshire Junction Railway, but by the time this postcard was published the line was jointly operated by the North British Railway and the Caledonian Railway under a grouping known as the Dumbarton & Balloch Joint Line Committee. PS *Princess May* had been built in 1898 and sailed on the loch until replaced by PS *Maid of the Loch* in 1953. That steamer is currently the subject of a continuing restoration project at Balloch Pier.

Empty stations were a feature of many railway cards – hardly a good advertisement for a successful railway.

Interestingly, the many railway companies seem to have been only too willing to give photographers access to their stations, so it is surprising they did not insist on there being evidence of activity.

A few miles away, at Aberfoyle, the picture was a little different. It is questionable whether or not there was ever really enough traffic to and from Aberfoyle to warrant the development of the Strathendrick & Aberfoyle Railway, which opened in 1882 extending the Blane Valley Railway to Aberfoyle.

Balloch Pier, Loch Lomond.

above: Aberfoyle Station was opened by the Strathendrick & Aberfolye Railway in 1882 and worked from the outset by the North British Railway, eventually being absorbed into the NBR in 1891.

The surviving postcards, however, paint a very positive picture, and suggest that, for a time at least, there must have been a considerable demand from tourist traffic.

Those routes which had successfully made it into the twentieth century seemed, by then, so much a part of the national fabric that they might endure forever. For a number of others, bankruptcies or takeovers had come almost as soon as laying the tracks had been completed. The Clydesdale

right: Taynuilt Station was opened by the Callander & Oban Railway when it extended services from Dalmally to Oban in 1880. From its inception the single line between Dalmally and Oban was worked using an electric token system, the first line in Britain to employ this safety feature. The line remains in use today.

Railway Station and Ben Cruachan, Taynuilt

Machrihanish Railway, Pier Head Station.

CAMPBELTOWN & MACHRIHANISH LIGHT · RAILWAY

TRAIN · LEAVES CAMPBELTOWN IMMEDIATELY· AFTER· PASSEN· ·GERS · HAVE · LANDED · FROM STEAMER.

TRAIN · LEAVES MACHRIHANISH FOR · CAMPBEL= TOWN. · AT 2 20 P.M.

MACHRIHANISH.

RETURN FARE 1/-

JOURNEY · TAKES 80 MINUTES EACH · WAY

TICKETS ISSUED ON STEAMER OR TRAIN

STEAMER WAITS RETURN OF TRAIN FROM MACHRIHANISH.

Junction Railway for example, established by Act of Parliament in 1845, was absorbed by the Caledonian Railway less than a year later – before it had even opened to traffic.

While locals did use the line, the majority of passengers alighting at Aberfoyle, or at nearby Callander, were met by fleets of horse-drawn charabancs for the journey to Loch Katrine's Trossachs Pier and a sail on the steamer – the SS *Rob Roy* until 1902, and thereafter the SS *Sir Walter Scott* which still sails the loch today. At least for this postcard c.1904, *opposite top*, the photographer waited for a train to arrive.

The Aberfoyle route was one of the first casualties of nationalisation in 1948, eventually closing in 1951 – yes, large parts of the Scottish railway network were being closed long before Dr Beeching wielded his axe in the 1960s. The station site, unsurprisingly, is now a car park.

The locomotive seen on the card, was North British Railways 'Class C' 0-6-0 No.359, designed in the 1870s by

above: The Campbeltown & Machrihanish Light Railway was a 2ft. 3ins. gauge line built to carry coal from Machrihanish to Campbeltown. It operated passenger services from 1908 until 1932, yielding to the growing popularity of the bus. The 0-6-2T *Argyll* was built by Andrew Barclay of Kilmarnock in 1906, the coaches by R. Y. Pickering of Wishaw in 1907.

above: Lenzie Station was opened as Kirkintilloch Junction in 1848 by the Edinburgh & Glasgow Railway. In 1849 it became Campsie Junction, changing to Lenzie Junction in 1867, the name shortened to Lenzie in 1890.

right: This 1904 card is captioned "This engine was built by Messrs J. & C. Carmichael of Dundee in 1833. It has a single driving wheel, and the cylinders, instead of being horizontal, are vertical and connected to the driving wheels by bell crank levers and connecting rods." It was built for the Dundee & Newtyle Railway.

Thomas Wheatley, built at Cowlairs, and already thirty years old by the time this picture was taken.

The importance of the railway in nineteenth and early twentieth century Scotland cannot be over-estimated and, although very few of the 146 independent companies which opened routes across the country ever showed a profit for their investors, they were central to Scotland's development – linking far flung communities and industries and, perhaps

most importantly, linking Scotland with the more populous centres south of the border.

Unlike several of their English counterparts, Scottish railway companies engaged much less with the idea of 'official' cards of their locomotives, rolling stock, and engineering departments at work. They did, of course, produce postcards of new locomotive designs throughout the Edwardian era. Postcards of stations, as in England, were largely produced by independent publishers.

There were, of course, the 'unofficial' postcards, few of which were ever widely published in the real sense of the word. By the middle of the Edwardian era, photographic

below left: Upper Greenock Station was opened in 1865 by the Greenock & Wemyss Bay Railway, but it proved a financial failure. The company never operated its own trains, services being run from the outset by the Caledonian Railway which eventually took the line over in 1893.

bottom: The Border Union Railway, a subsidiary of the North British Railway, started operating passenger services to and from Canonbie Station in 1862, three years after the line had been authorised. It was part of what became known as the 'Waverley Route' and from 1876 linked Edinburgh with Carlisle via the Midland Railway's Settle to Carlisle line. Canonbie station — known until 1904 as 'Canobie' — was closed when the line was axed in 1969 despite vociferous public protests.

UPPER GREENOCK STATION.

CANONBIE STATION.

Station, Crieff

above: An Edinburgh-bound train at Dalmeny Station c.1908 after crossing the Forth Bridge. The locomotive is either an NBR 'Class D' 0-6-0 designed by Matthew Holmes, or a Dugald Drummond designed 'Class C'.

right: Three minor railways – the Crieff Junction Railway, opened in 1856, the Crieff & Methven Junction Railway, opened in 1864 and the 1893 latecomer, the Crieff & Comrie Railway – all met at Crieff Junction. All three became part of the Caledonian Railway. The 'new' 1893 Caley Station with its 700ft platforms was closed in 1964.

companies such as Kodak sold boxes of postcard-sized photographic paper with pre-printed backs which conformed with current post office regulations. Several local photographers manufactured their own limited production-run postcards – hardly on a truly commercial scale – and posted those to their friends. Some even sold them in local shops.

'Disaster cards' were a feature of that market, with some dramatic cards produced by local photographers and publishers as well as national publishers in the days following the Gretna disaster at Quintinshill in May 1915. More than two hundred people – mainly troops – were killed due to a basic signaling error which caused a troop train to collide with two stationary trains.

Large commercial publishers exploited the disaster market as well. Valentines of Dundee, who became Scotland's largest postcard producer in Edwardian times, had operated as a commercial photographic studio since the 1860s producing scenic views for the expanding tourist market long before the

below: Loudon Hill Station, also known as Loudonhill, was on the Strathaven & Darvel Railway which was opened in 1905 and jointly run by the Glasgow & South Western Railway and the Caledonian Railway. This card, published by A. Morton, Stationer of Strathaven, was probably issued around the time of the line's opening and may have been the only Edwardian postcard of the station to be produced. The line itself was never a commercial success – nor probably was the postcard – closing before the beginning of the Second World War.

bottom: Cambuslang Station had been planned by the Clydesdale Junction Railway in 1845, but the company existed for little more than a year before being taken over by the Caledonian Railway. The station, on the line between Motherwell and Rutherglen, opened to traffic in June 1849.

Loudon Hill and Station. On the Strathaven and Darvel Railway
"The Avondale Series" Published by A. Morton, Stationer, Strathaven.

THE STATION CAMBUSLANG.

right: Published by
Valentine of Dundee
around a quarter of
a century after the
collapse of the Tay
Bridge in 1879, this
collage of fifty-four
ticket stubs collected
at St Fort Station
from some of the
passengers who lost
their lives, is one of
the most poignant
of railway 'disaster'
postcards. St Fort
Station was the
penultimate station
in Fife south of the
bridge, about half
way between
Leuchars and Wormit.
The actual death toll
remains uncertain to
this day, but probably
totalled 75. The poet
William McGonagall
claimed ninety
people died.

These Tickets were Collected at St Fort Station, on 28th December, 1879, by Robert Morris, Agent;
Wm. Friend, Ticket Collector; and Alex. Inglis, Porter, from the Passengers
who lost their lives by the Fall of the Tay Bridge.

83269

advent of the postcard. They had been ideally placed to
photograph the aftermath of the Tay Bridge Disaster in
December 1879.

A quarter of a century after the disaster itself – and
perhaps produced to commemorate that anniversary while
also satisfying the appetites of collectors – several of their
images were pulled out of the files and published as postcards
in 1904.

The card illustrated, *opposite*, even included *carte-de-visite* portraits of the train crew – portraits probably originally taken in Valentines' Dundee portrait studio.

There were a number of other disasters in the Edwardian period, including a major collision in 1906 at Elliot Junction between Carnoustie and Arbroath on the Dundee & Arbroath Joint Railway when 22 people died, including the local Liberal Member of Parliament.

The accident reportedly occurred in a blizzard when a North British Railway train collided with a D&AJR train standing at the station platform.

The North British driver was censured for ignoring warnings to drive with extreme caution due to the weather conditions. Local photographers were quickly on the scene, publishing postcard views of the aftermath, sales of which were probably predominantly local.

The majority of surviving disaster cards were never postally used, suggesting strongly that they were produced primarily for the growing numbers of Edwardian collectors rather than for actual use.

On the lighter side, while beautifully tinted postcards abound of rural Scottish stations, busy views of the main city centre stations in Edinburgh, Glasgow, Dundee and Aberdeen seem to be surprisingly uncommon. In assembling the images for this book, cards of major Scottish stations to match the bustling platforms and concourses of London Victoria, King's

below left: One of the carriages was still trapped inside the tangled wreckage of the fallen Tay Bridge section when the remains were raised from the river bed. Valentines of Dundee were ideally placed to photograph the recovered wreckage in 1879, pulling the pictures out of their files thirty years later for use on postcards clearly aimed at the collectors' market.

Tay Bridge Disaster, 1879.

DUNDEE

Some of many cards produced in the aftermath of the troop train disaster at Quintinshill near Gretna, May 22, 1915. Postcards of the disaster from five different publishers have so far been identified.

Wrecked Carriages, Gretna Green Railway Disaster May 22, 1915.

TERRIBLE TROOP TRAIN DISASTER.
ONE OF THE TELESCOPED CARRIAGES.

TERRIBLE TROOP TRAIN DISASTER.
One of the express engines telescoped on top of the wreckage of the troop train. The tender (on the left) has been thrown right over the side of the track.

South Beach Station.

Ardrossan.

South Beach Station.

Ardrossan.

above & left: Ardrossan's South Beach Station was opened in 1883 by the Glasgow & South Western Railway, on the line between Saltcoats and West Kilbride. Just north of the station, a branch line ran to the town's other two stations, Ardrossan Town and Ardrossan Harbour with its ferry crossings to Arran. The tinted card — based on the monochrome version, *left* — is a tribute to the art and craftsmanship of the postcard publishers.

Cross, Waterloo and Euston have proved elusive. Why this should be the case remains unexplained.

At the major coastal resorts, holidaymakers would have been the main purchasers of postcards, and the subject matter reflects that – postcards showing busy stations would be expected to sell in large numbers. The market for postcards at Ardrossan and Oban, for example, would have been considerable.

Two postcards of Oban Station, published before 1908. The station was opened by the Callander & Oban Railway in 1880 and enlarged in 1904 — the view above showing passengers disembarking from a train at one of the 'new' platforms. Although never formally part of the Caledonian Railway, all train services to Oban were operated by the CR. Despite having listed building status, the original station, *right*, was demolished in 1987, leaving the two 1904 platforms — still numbered 3 & 4 — for the six trains a day which connect with CalMac ferries to the Western Isles.

It is on cards like those that we see the art of the colourist at its finest, and where comparisons are possible, the realistic colour which they could create in their work is quite remarkable.

By the dawn of the postcard era, most of the 146 companies who had opened routes across Scotland had been consolidated into just five groupings – the Caledonian

Railway, the North British, The Great North of Scotland, the Glasgow & South Western, and the Highland, all of which survived until the creation of the 'big four' groups in 1923.

Each of the five had their own locomotive works – the Caledonian at St Rollox and the North British at Cowlairs, both in Glasgow, the Great North of Scotland at Inverurie, the Glasgow & South Western at Kilmarnock all continued building locomotives beyond the era covered by this book, while the Highland Railway's Lochgorm Locomotive Works in Inverness, always a much smaller scale operation, ceased production in 1906 having built just just over forty locomotives in its thirty-eight years of operation.

Last to roll off the production line at Lochgorm, in 1906, were four 'Class W' 0-4-4T locomotives designed by Peter Drummond.

Thereafter the Highland Railway sourced its locomotives from either Dübs & Company's Queens Park Works in Glasgow – who had been building locomotives for the company since 1874 – or the North British Locomotive Works in Springburn.

The Glasgow & South Western's Bonnyton Square Works in Kilmarnock built almost four hundred locomotives in its sixty-five year existence, but even that number pales into insignificance when compared with the thousands built at both the Caledonian and North British Glasgow works.

The Great North of Scotland Railway only started building their Inverurie Works north of Aberdeen in 1902, and only

below: A total of seventeen 240 class 4-4-0 express locomotives, designed by James Manson, were built by the Glasgow & South Western Railway at their Bonnyton Square locomotive works in Kilmarnock between 1904 and 1911.

Four coupled bogie Express, G. & S. W. R.   No. 447.

top: Highland Railway No.14 Yankee 4-4-0 tank engine was built by Dübs in Glasgow in 1893. Dübs had been contracted in 1891 to build five of these locomotives for Uruguay Railways but the order was cancelled after two had been built. They were bought by the Highland Railway who commissioned the other three with modifications to suit their needs. No.14, completed in November 1893 was one of those. The locomotive was renumbered 54 in 1901 – three years before this postard was published – and was briefly named *Portessie*. It was withdrawn from service in 1924, then carrying the LMS number 15017.

middle: This North British Railways 0-6-0ST had originally been built at Cowlairs in 1873, but is seen here after a major rebuild in 1902.

bottom: Built by Neilson & Reid for the Highland Railway, the 'Strath' Class 4-4-0 *Strathnairn* was a David Jones-designed passenger locomotive, one of 12 completed during a three month period in 1892. All were subsequently scrapped by the LMS before 1930.

ANNAN STATION G. & S. W.

The Station, Langbank.

left: Railway workers pose for the postcard photographer on the iconic Forth Bridge c.1908.

middle: Annan Station was on the route which extended south from the Glasgow, Paisley, Kilmarnock & Ayr Railway's line to New Cumnock. Opened by the Glasgow, Dumfries and Carlisle Railway in 1848, the line was operated from the start by the Glasgow & South Western Railway, and absorbed into the G&SWR in 1850. The G&SWR was formed from the merger of these two companies – GD&CR and the GPK&AR.

bottom: A four-coach train at Langbank Station between Port Glasgow and Bishopton in Renfrewshire c.1906, headed by McIntosh-designed Class 721 4-4-0 locomotive No.734, built by the Caledonian Railway at their St Rollox Works in Glasgow in 1896. Langbank Station had originally been opened as Lang Bank by the Glasgow, Paisley & Greenock Railway in 1841, before the PG&BR was absorbed into the Caledonian Railway in 1847.

top: The Caledonian Railway Class 49 locomotives, designed by John McIntosh, were built at the company's St Rollox Works in Glasgow in 1903. Just two were built, with five examples of a modified version – known as the Class 903 – coming out of St Rollox in 1906. All seven locomotives were rebuilt in 1911, and all subsequently carried the Class 903 classification. This postcard, from 'The Knight Series' was published by Knight Brothers Ltd. of London in 1906. Their catalogue of railway cards was extensive and although they were based on photographs, the over-painting on many obscured a lot of the fine detail of the original photograph.

right: A Caledonian Railway train, headed by Drummond 0-6-0 No.578, stands at the platform of Inverkip Station on the Greenock & Wemyss Bay Railway Company's line which was opened in 1865. The line was amalgamated with the Caledonian Railway in 1893.

LATEST EXPRESS ENGINE, CALEDONIAN RLY. (For Working Trains Between Carlisle And Glasgow.)

The Station,   Inverkip.

constructed ten locomotives on site – 4-4-0 Classes V and F tender engines, the first being out-shopped in 1906.

The great North British Locomotive Company in Glasgow survived into the post Second World War era – building steam locomotives well into the 1950s – but the advent first of diesel and then of electric heralded its decline. An attempted rescue plan in the late 1950s had only very limited success – largely due to the unreliability of many of the locomotives they built – and the company went into liquidation in 1962. A sad end for a company which had once built some of the world's finest steam engines.

For many years thereafter, the only builder of standard gauge locomotives in Scotland was Andrew Barclay in

Auldbar Road Station, near Letham

left: Auldbar Road Station, Letham, near Guthrie in Angus, was opened by the Arbroath & Forfar Railway in 1838, and originally laid to a 5ft 6ins gauge. Ten years later, the track was relaid to standard gauge in order to permit services to operate with the Aberdeen Railway Company. While services on the line were later shared by both the Caledonian Railway and the North British Railway, the Arbroath & Forfar Railway Company was never formally absorbed into either company and remained a separate entity until Grouping.

Kilmarnock which, after a series of takeovers now operates as a rolling stock repair facility.

Scotland's railway network today is a shadow of its former self with the Beeching axe alone responsible for the closure of 325 stations. Many more had closed decades earlier, but the growth in travel, and tourist interest in railways, has already seen several lines reopened over the past twenty years.

Perhaps the most significant development was the reconstruction of part of the famous Waverley Route – with steam trains once again running between Edinburgh and the Borders. Hopefully there will be more as demand increases further.

below left: A north-bound Caledonian Railway train standing at the up platform in Dunblane Station c.1906. The station had been established by the Scottish Central Railway in 1845, also becoming the terminus of the Dunblane, Doune & Callander Railway in 1846. By 1865, both companies had been absorbed by the Caley, and the station remains open today on the mainline between Stirling and Perth.

RAILWAY STATION DUNBLANE

top: Kirkcaldy Station was opened by the Edinburgh, Perth & Dundee Railway — originally planned as the Edinburgh & Northern Railway before a merger prior to the line's opening — in 1847. For a few years, the line formed a link between the ferry crossings on both the Forth and the Tay. By 1862 it was part of the North British Railway.

middle: Opened in April 1856 as a branch line terminus by the Perth & Dunkeld Railway, Dunkeld Station had, by 1863, become a through station when the Inverness & Perth Junction Railway — which had taken over the P&DR in 1862 — opened its line to Inverness via Pitlochry. Today, the 170 year old station buildings remain.

bottom: Castle Douglas Station in Dumfriesshire was opened in 1859 by the nominally independent Castle Douglas & Dumfries Railway which, while it constructed the line, never actually operated it. Running rights were vested in its parent company, the Glasgow & South Western Railway. The line closed to passenger services in 1965.

Kirkcaldy Station.

Dunkeld and Birnam Station

CASTLE DOUGLAS STATION.

The King's Visit to Blairgowrie, September 1908. His Majesty at Station

The King's Visit to Blairgowrie, September 1908 His Majesty at Station

King Edward VII boarding the Royal Train at Blairgowrie Station, September 1908. The Royal Visit had no specific purpose and was described as the King 'passing through' Blairgowrie, but it clearly warranted a guard of honour from the Black Watch as the King arrived at the branch line terminus where the Royal Train awaited. Other postcards from the series show the streets bedecked with bunting as the King's car swept past. The King had, earlier that day, unveiled the Victoria Memorial in Dunblane, and 'passed through' Coupar Angus and Rattray as well as Blairgowrie, each Burgh Council sending a letter of thanks to the Palace. Blairgowrie Station, was the terminus of a branch line from Coupar Angus on the Scottish Midland Junction Railway's line from Perth to Forfar, and had been opened in 1855. The company merged with the Aberdeen Railway in 1856 and by 1866 the enlarged company had become part of the Caledonian Railway. Passenger traffic on the Blairgowrie branch line ceased in 1955.

We will, however, never again see railways celebrated in anything approaching the rich variety of postcards which were published in the Edwardian era – there is simply no demand for them.

We now capture memories on our cameras or our phones, and transmit them instantaneously, but their major limitation is that, unlike the thousands of different postcards which celebrated the heyday of Scotland's – and Britain's – railways, those photographs will not survive to be marvelled at and enjoyed by future generations a century and more after they were published. That enjoyment is, without doubt, one of the reasons we become collectors.

INDEX